The Divinity of Mankind

Part I

Revelations of Mary, Jesus and Mary Magdalene

For our parents Bouwe and Grietje, Samuel and Julia

We thank Geertje, Pieter, Micha, Henk, Ineke, Jan, Marijke, Marijke, Anne-Sabine, Jeannette, Ria, Sunny, Milenko, Milica and Marjan for their support and valuable advice.

The Divinity of Mankind

Part 1

Revelations of Mary, Jesus and Mary Magdalene

Gabriela and Reint Gaastra-Levin

Follow Your Heart Publishing - Apeldoorn, the Netherlands

Contents

lective interests into balance and focus on love, care and compassion, are they able to make contact with extraterrestrial forms of consciousness. *Prayer to experience Divinity in all forms of life.*

in the heart. Exercises: 'Each day of your life is a movie', 'We love the Earth' and 'Beliefs about death'.

Exercise for the integration of all people and other forms of consciousness to create a network of love and light.

Revelation 22

The spiritual masters emphasise the personal transformation of the people who wish to participate in the Christ Project and the development of their consciousness. They explain that the various religions actually complement each other and will all have a place in the new community. "Do you think that Mohammed, Jesus, Buddha and Moses could be in struggle with each other?" Exercise to accept other religions.

Revelation 23

The spiritual masters emphasise the importance of improved inter-action between the 'highest' and 'lowest' chakras in our bodies in order to actually be able to experience the power of love and the Divine. Basic principles for participating in the Christ Project are formulated. Exercise to put negative opinions into perspective.

Revelation 24

Mary and Jesus compare the parent/child relationship with the relationship between the spiritual masters and mankind. If a parent fosters his or her inner child, that parent is also better able to give his or her child love and acknowledge that child as an individual soul. Mankind has achieved increased consciousness and reveals itself more and more as a partner of the spiritual masters. Exercise to make contact with your inner child and to accept it.

Revelation 25

Mary and Jesus tell about the special relationship between the spiritual masters and mankind. The spiritual masters occasionally wonder whether they should 'save' people from the situations in life that they themselves have created or whether they should let them fully experience these situations from the point of view of the evolutionary process. The answer is provided by the Divine plan. It is time for people to take responsibility for what they create and learn to make other choices. Mankind and the masters can then be partners. Exercise as an aid for consciously deciding whether or not you want to be a victim in this life.

Foreword by the authors

Dear Readers,

We hadn't been together for very long when we were 'visited' by the spiritual masters in the year 2000. The most suitable and quiet moment for contact turned out to be during prayers before our hot meal at noon. After recovering from our initial surprise, the first messages came through to Gabriela from Mary, Jesus and Mary Magdalene. This was a very special, wondrous and poignant moment. They asked explicitly whether we would make ourselves available for passing on a book that was to bear the title "The Divinity of Mankind – Revelations of Mary, Jesus and Mary Magdalene".

We started on the 'conveyance sessions' in our study at the end of August 2000 after an enervating visit to Jerusalem during the summer of that same year, just prior to the serious clashes between the Palestinians and the Jews. We were most honoured. With candles lit and pictures of Jesus and Mary around us, Gabriela 'received' the first Revelations. She voiced them and Reint recorded what 'came through' on his personal computer. We both opened ourselves to this special contact. We also communicated back and forth on a regular basis whenever we explicitly requested, and received, additional information and clarification from the masters (both male and female) who said that they belonged to the White Brother- and Sisterhood. Because we were often too busy with our day-to-day affairs, the information came through at intervals over a period of two years. It was simply a matter of planning time in our schedules, saying an opening prayer and performing a ritual at the agreed time to make ourselves as available as possible, and Mary, Jesus and/or Mary Magdalene tuned into us to make contact and convey their knowledge.

It sounds simple, but it was not always easy, especially in the beginning. The innovative messages we were permitted to receive for mankind often 'came through' so passionately that we sometimes had to break off after only fifteen minutes because we were so 'moved'. In point of fact, we both found ourselves in a radical transformation process in which we were confronted with our convictions and assumptions and our 'disbelief' that stood in the way of our actually accepting the Divine Revelations. These obstacles within ourselves first had to be removed before we could open ourselves completely to the glorious messages.

Gradually, the sessions became easier and we were better able to surrender ourselves to them. 'Writing' these Revelations was a revelation in itself, but also a struggle. On the one hand, it was both intense and interesting to be allowed to receive these marvellous insights; on the other hand, we were constantly amazed that we had been singled out to do so. But we also asked ourselves: "What effect will this have on our lives and our relationships? Will people have intense reactions to us?"

At a certain stage, after having been requested over and over again to make ourselves available, we decided to 'go for it' unconditionally and in complete confidence. The book then practically wrote itself. We are now proud and delighted to present it to you; we stand behind its entire contents.

Our relationship with Mary, Jesus and Mary Magdalene has stirred us deeply. The masters show us our 'limitations', but also our Divinity. The latter is often more difficult to accept than the former. Sometimes we do not let ourselves be touched completely by their love. And we have a kind of fear – a fear to admit and to acknowledge our true Divine essence and our connection with the higher dimensions. At the same time all the messages, prayers and exercises, for which we are most grateful, have filled us with inspiration and joy. They elevate us to our true nature. We would like to take you on a journey back to the Divine roots of mankind. A journey meant for all of us. May this book be our guide.

Gabriela and Reint Gaastra-Levin
Apeldoorn, the Netherlands - November 2002

Foreword by Mary, Jesus and Mary Magdalene

Dear people on Earth,

First of all, please let us thank you for all the love and dedication you have given us during the past two thousand years. About two thousand years ago, a major transformation occurred in the hearts of humans and on Earth in which we played an important part. Mankind was ready for it. Through our interaction with man we too have grown in our development, for which we are grateful. Throughout the years we have remained in contact with mankind. We have supported the human processes and development. You have gone through a lot over the centuries. Now it is time to reap the harvest. Mankind is entering a new phase and so are we. For you, this has to do with an awakening of the Christ-consciousness in your hearts, the embodiment of unconditional Divine love. For us, as mankind takes over more of our tasks on Earth, it means that we can connect and collaborate more with extraterrestrial light beings and that we will concentrate more on Earth's connection with the universe.

Mankind is ready to embrace the Christ-energy in their hearts. The Christ-energy is a source of bliss, connection and creativity. There is a lot to do on Earth. You are ready for a transformation of all the forms that the human existence on Earth has assumed up to now. Because although you have occupied yourselves all these years with religious norms and values, an essential piece of the puzzle has been missing and that is your own Divine nature, your Divinity. This insight will change the way humans view life. This essential basic principle is lacking in practically all the creations of the current human civilisation. As soon as you accept this truth, your hearts will open and you will discover that society does not reflect this essence. And then you will have the need to transform your houses, buildings, relationships, communication models, economy, politics and all other aspects that belong to the human existence into forms that better reflect your Divinity.

During the past two thousand years you have occupied yourselves with us and with a limited version of our teachings. For several reasons, these teachings lacked certain essential aspects, such as the Divine essence of all that exists and of man in particular, the equality of man and woman, the presence of the Christ-energy in all your hearts, the possibility of man to be a master, the purity of human conception and a series of other aspects that you will encounter when reading this book.

In the course of time you have created and shaped an incomplete picture of us. We feel that that picture needs to be clarified. The time is now right. You will discover new aspects while reading our Revelations. Open yourself to them and let them into your heart. Trust your intuition and give yourself space and time to integrate these new messages into your life on this beautiful planet Earth. Say the prayers with respect as often as possible as dictated by the heart so that you can feel our presence and energy. Do the exercises intensively, demurely and conscientiously so that they can help you open your heart to enable you to become more and more your real self on Earth. This will bring us ever closer together.

In love and unity,

Mary, Jesus and Mary Magdalene

Foreword by the White Brother- and Sisterhood

Dear people on Earth,

You may wonder who we are. We are a group of spiritual masters (both male and female) who have already experienced all human dilemmas of existence in countless incarnations and who have completed all learning phases on Earth as humans. We are able to look upon you with compassion from a broader perspective and a higher dimension, so that we can help you on both an individual and a collective level to build a bridge between your Divinity and your personalities in your various lives on Earth.

We have been incarnated in various cultures and at various times in the history of man. We have experienced all the different aspects of human existence in several lives and have disengaged ourselves from them. We have outgrown human illusions and have raised ourselves above human experiences by experiencing and accepting them and by giving them their own place. We have discovered that the apparent happiness that every human experience offers is only temporary. True happiness lies in accepting who we are in essence, in radiating our Divinity and in our connection with the unconditional love of the heart. This is how we were able to disengage and become serene. This placed us above the duality of material, emotional, rational and other contrasts, above 'choosing sides', above 'having the last word'; it allowed us to accept all aspects of Earthly life and all human experiences. We are now full of compassion and joy, have let go of 'the struggle' and enjoy the Divine 'game', all manifestations of life on Earth and the human existence in particular. We are spiritual powers that represent various aspects of God.

We were incarnated once and recognised and acknowledged by you as Buddha, Lao Tse, Mary, Jesus, Mary Magdalene, Confucius, John, Rabbi Shimon, Sri Aurobindo, Zarathustra and many other masters.

We have waited a long time to make contact with man in this way. We have inspired and guided you in the background from the spiritual world throughout the centuries. As your awareness grew, communication with you became increasingly stronger. The more you opened your hearts, the more you turned to us for inspiration and guidance. The more you turned to us, the more we were allowed to support you in finding the Divine spark in yourself.

Mankind has now reached the stage that it is able to take responsibility for its own Divinity, just like we and everything else that exists are Divine. We can enter into this new phase together with joy. It is a new period in which man takes centre stage, in which you will bring, to an increasing extent, the action and words of the heart into the material world. And you will more and more often proclaim and live up to the message of unconditional love and allow your love for yourself and others. This will result in a new order on Earth with even greater and deeper love and brotherhood – love and sisterhood that are based on your love for yourself, or in other words, the healing of the individual that ultimately results in the healing of society. People can finally also love themselves. The love for yourself cures all the old spiritual wounds, which then no longer need to be projected and vented on society. If people feel peace and love in their hearts, peace and love will develop in society; this is an essential piece of the puzzle that may soon be whole. The healing of the individual, of the relationships with family and friends and of society will again enable this planet to connect more consciously with the cosmic order to which Earth belongs. The fulfilment that this connection brings about will create a new wave of bliss on Earth inspiring the people to come together in united awareness; the ultimate human experience of being Divine.

We, the White Brother- and Sisterhood, of whom particularly Mary, Jesus and Mary Magdalene address you in this book, stand ready to give you even deeper, clearer and more devoted guidance in this phase, partly enabled by your personal growth. It is for this purpose that the three of them give you this book. Feel free to seek direct contact with them in stillness or in the passion of your heart. They can be approached at all times and in any way. You will feel their answer in your heart.

Mankind has arrived at a special time in its development. You are on the verge of discovering the illusion of duality. More and more people want to see the whole truth and are no longer satisfied with part of the truth. You no longer believe in a struggle against a possible evildoer and believe less and less in the existence of victims and offenders. Mankind is about to experience and to acknowledge its own Divinity and to take complete responsibility for all its own creations on Earth. This can be compared to the end of the adolescent phase after which one enters adulthood and stands on one's own two feet. May this book contribute to your process of awakening, liberation and transformation so that Divine love can manifest itself on Earth from the human heart.

Together in the heart,

The White Brother- and Sisterhood

How to use this book

'The Divinity of Mankind – Revelations of Mary, Jesus and Mary Magdalene' is not the kind of book you read from beginning to end without putting it down. The Revelations are often so innovative and 'out of the ordinary' that you will need some time to digest them and give them a place in your heart and realm of thought. You may have some difficulty with certain chapters because they affect you personally and might lead you into a personal process. Take your time. Skip these chapters if necessary and come back to them later when the book has become a part of you.

Experience proves that readers develop a bond with the book in their own particular way; they look for and develop their own method to benefit fully from the book, to enjoy it and to continue to be amazed.

So it is not a book to be approached purely from a rational point of view. It is above all an exercise book and 'feel' book. By practicing the exercises and prayers you will 'sense' or 'feel' a clearer picture of yourself, connect with the spiritual world and create an atmosphere and an energy of the heart that substantiate your own Divinity and open your heart so that you become an increasingly more loving person for yourself, for your fellow man and for the world.

The Exercises

The purpose of the exercises proffered by Mary, Jesus and Mary Magdalene is for you to gain insight into yourself and to gradually open your heart. To achieve this, you can best do the exercises with your eyes closed unless stated otherwise. Closing your eyes automatically puts you in touch with your deeper spiritual levels. It would be wonderful if you had a 'buddy' with whom you could take turns doing the exercises. This buddy can help you by reading the exercises out loud at a speed you feel comfortable with. You can signal how fast or slow you want to go by a gesture of the hand or by nodding your head, for instance. You can agree on some signals in advance so that the person who is doing the exercise can remain in the depths of his or her experience whilst indicating the pace.

Should you not be able to find or should you not want a companion, you can record the various steps of the exercises on a cassette tape at a leisurely pace and then coach yourself by means of the tape. Another option is to record your reactions and emotions on a separate tape while doing the exercises. You can also do this when you work with a buddy.

The publisher of this book is planning to record the exercises on a compact disk, which can be ordered, when available, for a small consideration. Relevant information is provided on our website: www.divinityofmankind.com.

The exercises initiate a process of awakening that can unfold during the days and weeks after doing the exercises. This process continues its work in your consciousness. You will notice that the exercises will pop up regularly in your mind during your daily activities.

Follow your own intuition to determine the order and frequency of the exercises. Share your experiences and insights with others. Inspire others to examine and develop themselves. Let others inspire you. Your individual growth is also linked to teamwork.

The Prayers

The prayers provide the link and connect us with our spiritual friends. Use them for everything that you do, wish and experience from your heart. Be uninhibited in this. Pray as often as possible. Praying opens your heart and introduces a pleasant high vibration into your life and into the lives of others. Pray often for yourself and often for others. Pray regularly for our planet and for mankind. By praying you raise the collective consciousness of mankind to a higher level. Share the prayers with others; do not keep them to yourself. Share what you experience through the prayers with them too. Inspire others to use them as well or to pray in their own way.

We recommend that you make notes of what you experience in order to track your developments over time. Focus your attention completely when saying the prayers. Feel every word and allow every word to penetrate. Pray as much as possible at a leisurely pace. This will enable the prayers to touch deeper levels within yourself. Keep still for a moment after each prayer to feel the effect of the prayer within yourself.

After getting up in the morning and before going to bed at night are ideal moments to pray. Before having a meal, it is also nice to dwell, through prayer, upon the useful role that other beings fulfil in your life and to be thankful for it. Your heart will open even further. In this way you will receive the spiritual nutrition that the life forms you consume wish to give to you. This way we may receive their unconditional love.

The prayers can be found throughout the book in the various Revelations. To make them more accessible during your daily activities, they are repeated at the back of the book in larger print for copying. This makes them easy to carry about with you. Or you can leave them on your bedside table, for instance, or any other familiar place where you can easily pick them up at regular intervals.

The Revelations

The Revelations in the book are in a specific order intended to take you by the hand on your journey within yourself. However, you may feel compelled to read them in a different order. Feel free to do so; it makes your inner journey more personal.

It may be that, while reading a particular Revelation, you feel you must stop because – as physical reactions indicate – you have entered into a process within yourself. In this case it is advisable to close your eyes and 'descend into the depths'. Take all the time you need and allow yourself sufficient leeway; it is an integral part of the process. The book is intended to occupy a place in your life so that it can stimulate your inner transformation as fully as possible.

Revelation 1

The spiritual masters communicate their responsibility for Earth on an intergalactic level in collaboration with mankind. Every individual is jointly responsible for activating the Divine spark on Earth. Energetic forms of consciousness are a part of this process. The effect of the crucifixion of Jesus on Earth's aura. List of questions of the spiritual masters for getting people into a personal spiritual process to help them connect more easily with each other.

Mary, Jesus, Mary Magdalene and other masters in the White Brother- and Sisterhood: "We look at Earth from the outside. We have an interest in Earth. We are able to see and feel Earth's aura, its field of energy. We are able to see and experience the relationship between Earth and the Cosmos. We are aware of this relationship and also of the cosmic processes on Earth. So we observe from this wider perspective. It provides a different frame of reference. Most people who function on Earth do not see this context and it is our task to create a link between their processes and this cosmic framework. Everyone on Earth carries a Divine spark within but is not always aware of this fact. Because you are so focussed on daily events you are often in a kind of semi-conscious state. Sometimes shocks are required to wake you up: events that turn everyday life upside down. Such as in the time of the solar eclipses or during certain natural disasters, social crises, wars, a panic on the stock exchange. Then you sit up and take notice and you suddenly see developments on Earth in a wider context. And the Divine spark is activated."

Mankind and spiritual helpers together

"Everyone is able to take steps in their own awakening process. We hereby call upon you to 'wake up'. We have an immense shared task, namely to manifest the Christ-consciousness in every person on Earth. We do this together. It is not exclusively your task, nor ours. We are implementers belonging to a much greater intergalactic order that supervises developments in awareness at a cosmic level. This order affords a harmonious and evolutionary policy with respect to tasks such as the migration of souls from one planetary system to another, the proper balance between various galaxies and solar systems, the exchange of awareness developments between various galaxies, coordinating genetic improvements, exchanging experiences at ecological and social levels, carrying out and coordinating projects – such as the project Planet Earth –, the distribution and reproduction of various life forms and species, monitoring various awareness zones, monitoring the well-being of and the care for various life forms, monitoring and providing a link between all sorts of life forms and the Almighty. This organisation has various levels of responsibility and tasks. The responsibilities are distributed perfectly. Each subsystem has its own management body that provides a link with the great intergalactic order (see the Glossary) and that adapts the tasks of the great intergalactic order to the order of the subsystem, for instance a solar system."

Every human being also bears responsibility

"The various hierarchies mentioned above are reflected in every one of you. The aspects and tasks of the intergalactic order are repeated on a small scale throughout this solar system. There is an intensive exchange system between the various planets themselves and the Sun. We, the White Brother- and Sisterhood (see our foreword) are responsible for the connection between Earth and the cosmic order. The Earth is a planet whose importance extends beyond the solar system. The importance of Earth is linked to an even greater project, namely allowing man to experience the free-will zone and investigating whether man is able to become aware of his own Divine nature, after this has descended into matter and been incarnated on Earth. The importance of this process impacts the entire universe. If you are able to make a success of this project, you will lift the entirety to a new dimension. If you do not succeed, Creation will undergo additional evolutionary cycles in order to solve this crisis. Everyone must be aware of his or her own responsibility in this. Yet both possibilities are a part of the Divine 'game'; both roads ultimately lead to the same end result."

"What will happen if you do succeed? Succeeding means that you will regain the experience of your Divinity. It means that you have the intention to let go of everything necessary to return to your heart. That you choose to open your heart to yourself, to your fellow man and to everything on Earth, to see through all sorts of power games and to connect lovingly with others. This is a process that starts on a small scale, in your own life, in your relationship towards yourself and your fellow man and in relation to society and the world. It begins with yourself. You will realise that it is a unique opportunity for every soul to occupy a human body and to live on Earth. But this is also accompanied by responsibilities."

Other forms of consciousness

"Earth is currently in a state of flux. It is drawing near to a period of cleansing and purification. As a being, it has made itself available for this project and has been willing to provide physical forms for various kinds of souls, such as plants, animals and people. It has now come to a point of suffering because it senses how you treat each other and nature."

"However, there are other forms of intelligence and consciousness that have linked their evolutionary processes to that of mankind, making this evolutionary process even more complex. Examples of these forms of consciousness are energetic entities that are created and/or fed by collective emotions and thoughts and energetic forms of consciousness that come to us from other places in the universe. They are fed by aggression, hard-heartedness, confusion and fear and they kindle these forces. These forms of consciousness must contend with something on Earth, just like you. They have a certain influence on the development of mankind; you nourish them unwittingly. These forms become involved and feel committed when you call on them, however subtly. You do this through thoughts, wishes and statements."

"These thoughts, wishes and statements can attract either supportive powers or destructive forces. If you have negative thoughts towards someone you unwittingly call in certain invisible energetic entities that want to feed on aggression. You both tune into a certain wavelength, an awareness frequency, just like tuning into a radio station. In a manner of speaking, you switch on Radio Violence or Radio Love. By tuning into this wavelength you nourish that frequency, as it were. When millions of people engage in violence every day, each at their own level and in all forms imaginable, no matter how subtle, a violent field of energy is created that can manifest itself in the shape of wars, natural disasters or accidents. Everyone on Earth is jointly responsible for all processes, both good and bad. If you regularly tune in to love, then it is this frequency that is nourished and stimulated."

"By meditating and praying on a regular basis, you create an added source of light that will help matters tremendously. If you transform tension and discord in yourself as well, you will give your Divine spark increasingly greater leeway and you will contribute significantly to the collective process and to your own growth. Our message is: 'Become aware of your Divine spark. Learn how you function and discover what influence you have on your surroundings and vice versa.'"

Jesus' time on Earth was important

"A very important process took place in the time of Jesus Christ. A group of highly evolved souls arrived on Earth to open up the way for the Christ-energy. Some acted in a human body, some operated from a subtle level. We, the White Brother- and Sisterhood, came together at that time to participate in the history of mankind in a recognisable physical form. Mary, Jesus, Mary Magdalene, Joseph and John are examples of this. Every one of us had a specific role. Everything was according to the Divine plan. While Jesus was being crucified a tremendous amount of light poured out from the purest energy level of the Almighty onto Earth (see also Revelation 20), raising Earth's aura to a higher vibration and increasing the awareness of mankind."

Appeal and questions for man

"We would very much like you to cooperate with us. Start on the exercises contained in this book. Focus on yourself. By means of these questions we would like to encourage you to think of yourself and to work on yourself. It is our intention to start up a process that will bring you closer to your heart and that will tune you in to the light you carry in your heart. And to improve your relationships so that you can get closer to others and commit yourself to a greater extent. It is ultimately all about the connecting force of love. Love for yourself, love for others and love for God."

"Take a good look at the following questions and let them sink in. Become aware of the feelings that each question arouses in you. Note down your answers on a separate sheet of paper.

• Do you have complaints of a physical nature?
• Is your lifestyle a healthy one?
• Do you feel good?
• Do you get enough rest?

- Do you feel any emotional stress?
- Are there any sources of inner pain and sorrow in your life?
- Are you happy?
- How are your relationships?
- Are your relationships supportive or restrictive?
- Are you a supportive or a restrictive factor for others?
- How do you contribute to society? Are you interested in social processes? Do they move you?
- Do you follow your calling?
- Does your work make you happy?
- Do you follow your heart?

If you wish, you can keep these notes so that you can compare them with the answers you give at a later date should you feel the need to ask yourself these questions again."

Revelation 2

Mary, Jesus and Mary Magdalene talk about the Divine team of mankind's spiritual helpers. Man's choice between spiritual freedom and conditioning. The need dictated by one's ego to be unique isolates man, removing this need unifies man. Exercises with regard to the purpose of going through experiences during life on Earth.

Mary, Jesus, Mary Magdalene: "In this Revelation we would like to share certain aspects with you as to the reason for our involvement with Earth. You sometimes think that the Earth is an isolated planet in the universe. This is not true. The various processes on Earth are monitored closely by higher forces of consciousness, such as guides, spiritual masters and angels. Yet the Earth is a free-will zone, which means that the souls that incarnate on Earth are given the opportunity to make their own choices within their development process. The extent to which these choices are truly free is a different matter. You see, you are also very conditioned. By conditioned we mean that you may think you are making your own decisions out of your own free will, but your thinking is controlled by assumptions, convictions and awareness patterns without you realising it. Examples of this phenomenon are genetic conditioning (hereditary characteristics), karmic conditioning (lessons out of this life and former lives that you must still complete), collective conditioning (traditions that restrict awareness and that cause such epidemics as foot-and-mouth disease, mad cow disease and swine fever), ecological conditioning (the impact of environmental pollution on health) and even extraterrestrial conditioning (the influence of forms of consciousness from other stars and planets on the developments on Earth of which you are not yet aware). Still, the soul has a certain amount of free will within all these conditionings."

Conditioning or spiritual freedom?

"The most essential decision is whether you want to strengthen this conditioning or whether you opt for your own freedom. This is often a very subtle choice, sometimes even confusing. But what is so confusing? You often think that you are making free choices, but ultimately your decisions are based on conditioning or vice versa. In order to distinguish between the two we recommend that you feel this issue with the heart and follow the heart. The heart unites you again, brings you back to the love for yourself and others; brings you peace and happiness. The opposites of these are your ego's fears. The ego thinks it must survive. The ego knows deep down that its existence is only temporary. The fear of survival and the need to manifest itself in everyday life are two essential aspects of the ego. Simply stated, the ego is a trick of evolution. It is a Divine tool created to give your 'higher self' a material base. After the soul has incarnated in the material human being, it suddenly feels isolated. Connected with this is the need to be unique, the need to manifest oneself. Letting go of the need to be unique is the first step towards freedom. The need to be unique isolates you, removing this need puts you in touch with each other and with creation in its entirety. In first instance, incarnation leads to isolation; unification is the way back to the Divine. You are somewhere in the middle of this process. An upward spiral can be discerned towards better contact, both with each other and with nature, the cosmic order and the Divine forces. Humanity is on its way back to the Divine. It is our intention to help you let go of the superfluous mental deadwood that you have collected over the centuries. It is a matter of breaking through the wall you have built up around your ego; a wall made of bricks of fear, anger, ignorance, impotence, sorrow and despair. This opens you up to love for yourself and for others, to faith and compassion. Yet you continue to add new bricks to that wall, while the heart tries to remove them. And it is precisely for this reason that you can call upon us. We are available for this; it is our calling. It is what this book is intended for. The creation of the ego as well as letting go of the ego is a Divine process; the one cannot exist without the other."

Being unique in solidarity

"In order to let go of something you must first have been able to experience these aspects of life on Earth. If you experience something to the full you have the opportunity of getting the best out of what you are seeking in that experience and at the same time of becoming aware of the limitations of the experience. Through your experiences of life you ultimately seek the way back to unity. And every time again, you discover that experiencing unity is not so much a matter of going through the experience, but of letting go of the experience. Because the more you can keep yourself detached while experiencing something, the more you can be keenly sensible of the ultimate in the experience. These two levels can grow towards one another. This process occurs in waves; it is a natural process, which means that it cannot be forced. You cannot let go of certain experiences until you are ready to do so. For example, letting go of consuming meat and then constantly thinking of steaks gives you an unsatisfactory experience. So it is better to continue eating meat for a few more years until you have completed that experience. It works perfectly. As each soul gradually frees itself from the illusions of matter it experiences deeper and new bonds with souls that are also in a similar process. This leads to an evolutionary acceleration process with new opportunities. You gradually become aware of the two sides of this process, namely being unique in solidarity. As this self-knowledge, this awareness grows, being unique becomes less important for the soul in question and is replaced by a developing process towards unity and solidarity until at some stage the heart becomes totally unselfish and unconditional. And that is the Christ-consciousness."

Exercises about experiencing

"The purpose of the following exercises is to help you reflect on the value and purpose of 'going through experiences' during life on Earth. By looking at and appreciating the experiences free of any deadwood, you can make deliberate decisions about what you want to experience and you can gain insight into what you have already completed. Fulfilling a certain need is the main motivation for the experience of life. Recognising whether you actually get satisfaction is the basis for making a deliberate decision whether to continue or to complete the experience."

Exercise 1 – Completed experiences

"Draw up a list of experiences you are done with. Being done with an experience means that you no longer have any need to look for and go through an experience like that. Incidentally, all experiences are useful. Look at them objectively with total acceptance, even experiences that are painful. Answer the following questions for each experience you have listed.

• What was the need for which you sought fulfilment by gaining this experience?

• Has this need been fulfilled or are you still seeking fulfilment?

• How does that feel?

• What have you learned from these experiences?"

Exercise 2 – Still uncompleted experiences

"Draw up a list of experiences you are not yet done with. All experiences are useful. Look at them objectively with total acceptance, even experiences that are painful. Answer the following questions for each experience you have listed.

• What is the need for which you seek fulfilment by means of this experience?

• Has this need been fulfilled or are you still seeking fulfilment?

• How does that feel?

• Are there reasonable possibilities for fulfilling your need through these experiences?
If so, enjoy them until you feel you are done with them (and you can cross off the experience). If not, will you accept the fact and let the experience go?"

Revelation 3

Mary provides insight into mankind's connection with the Cosmos. The manner in which man functions influences how the Cosmos functions and vice versa. Only when people bring personal and collective interests into balance and focus on love, care and compassion, are they able to make contact with extraterrestrial forms of consciousness. Prayer to experience Divinity in all forms of life.

Mary: "People are created as mirrors of the Cosmos. Every part of a human being is a manifestation of the whole. Each human cell contains a complete blueprint of the entire person. Similarly, everybody has, within him- or herself, a complete blueprint of the universe; hence the significance of the saying "Know thyself!". How you treat yourself influences the universe. This can be compared to treatments that are applied to one part of the body, but that in fact affect the entire body, such as reflex zone therapy or acupuncture. You are ready to become aware of your role in the universe. You have shirked this responsibility by thinking that the beings on Earth are the only living beings in the universe. This is absolutely not true. The universe is fully inhabited at all levels of consciousness; it is filled with manifestations of consciousness. Some forms of consciousness opt for a life in a three-dimensional form, such as a soul that manifests itself as an incarnation in a human being."

Personal and collective interests in balance

"You have not yet discovered or have not yet had contact with other forms of life and consciousness in the universe. This is because mankind's consciousness decreased collectively during the last five thousand years before Christ – a decline that was put back on its way to recovery with the birth of Jesus Christ. There is a self-protecting mechanism in the universe that is triggered when a particular civilisation is not able to deal responsibly with its own powers; mainly when personal interest rises above the common good. The latter two interests should be in balance. Only when one is able to place personal interests second to a civilisation's collective interest and the collective is at the same time able to care for the individual, only then will the civilisation gain access to other universal levels of consciousness. I do not mean to say that the individual is not important or that individuals must sacrifice themselves and may not care for themselves. What I am explaining here is a process in which a human being takes primary responsibility for his or her own development. At some stage in this development process you discover your own heart and in the flow of love you experience from the heart you realise you are not alone. At a certain point you experience happiness as a result of the happiness of others. Then a process of awakening begins that makes you realise that you can mean something to each other and that your behaviour can be of added value to the life of others and vice versa. Realising this interaction is a leap forward in human consciousness."

Contact with other forms of consciousness

"When human beings create conflicts among themselves, people take it out individually on their surroundings. This is one of the reasons why, in this day and age, the environment suffers so severely and why wars still break out. Earth is your playground, but your conflicts are so fierce that the entire universe is affected by their consequences. You do not realise it yet, but everything that happens on Earth has its impact on the universe. That is why certain protective mechanisms are in force. For instance, certain technologies are not always accessible to mankind because your worldly consciousness has not yet developed to a level that allows you to deal with them with respect and in a holistic way.

"When love and compassion have become the most important values on Earth, you will be able to solve the most basic problems. Problems like poverty, disease and hunger do not belong to a 'developed civilisation'. Compare this with the process of an individual who deals with his or her basic needs with compassion, understanding and attention. That person is able to care for himself or herself with love. In a similar way, an entire civilisation is able to maintain itself. Contact with the countless life forms in the universe can then be restored. You will then treat these forms of life and consciousness with respect. If you were to come into contact with them now, many of you would still tend to be selfish or destructive in your association with these forms, as all sorts of life forms on Earth already experience today. Positive developments with respect to ecology are taking place, but there is still a long way to go."

First heal mankind

"Mankind on Earth will first have to be healed before it is granted access to the universe on a larger scale. Earth is a major point of special attention for the cosmic community; countless processes are taking place around the planet. Various extraterrestrial civilisations also incorporate certain aspects of their development into their relationship with Earth. The White Brother- and Sisterhood (see their foreword) are very much involved in the process of human development on Earth. We have assumed the responsibility to inspire you and to remind you of your Divine nature. This is done layer by layer, step by step. Like a child that must learn to stand and then walk, we take you by the hand in this process of awakening."

Prayer — All is Divine and one

"The purpose of this prayer is to recognise Divinity in all life forms. Find a place where you cannot be disturbed. Light a candle and make yourself comfortable. Repeat the following prayer to yourself and then remain quiet for a while."

Dear Heavenly Father
And all the unconditional guides, masters, angels and higher souls of the universe,
I feel, look at and listen to you with all due love and respect
Because I know
That we have been created out of the same Divine love.
We are one!

Dear Heavenly Mother
And all gentle powers of the universe
And Mother Nature
With all her plants, animals and creatures,
I feel, look at and listen to you with all due love and respect
Because I know
That we have been created out of the same Divine love.
We are one!

Dear brothers and sisters of the universe,
Of all the stars and planets and various dimensions,
I feel, look at and listen to you with all due love and respect
Because I know
That we have been created out of the same Divine love.
We are one!

Dear people
Who are together here on Earth,
I feel, look at and listen to you with all due love and respect
Because I know
That we have been created out of the same Divine love.
We are one!

Dear Heavenly Mother and Father,
Dear brothers and sisters of the universe,
Dear people on Earth,
We are one!
Amen

Revelation 4

Mankind's attention is drawn to the fact that it must assume responsibility for its own Divinity. People can become aware that they are the creators of their own reality. Jesus explains that we are all a trinity: every person is both father (creator), son (creation) and Holy Spirit (creative power). To make contact with the spiritual world, people are invited to pray. But what is a prayer? Mary, Jesus and Mary Magdalene provide essential prayers to invoke them. Mary explains in detail the significance of the prayer addressed to her.

Mary, Jesus and Mary Magdalene: "While reading this book and after you have finished it, you may ask yourself how it is possible to make and maintain contact with the spiritual Divine world. You may think it is a very rare phenomenon only meant for the elect. You are convinced of this because you have been trained not to consider yourself Divine but to look up to the Divine. In this way you wrong both yourself and God. You deny your own Divine essence and blame God that the Divine power is not available to you. By looking upon yourself in this way, you deprive yourself of your own Divine power. The time has come to put aside this assumption and open yourself up to your own essence. This entails a certain responsibility. 'Take responsibility for your own Divinity!' This means that you no longer walk around on Earth as lost creatures and nurse the feeling that you are a victim of your own fate, but that you are the creator of your own reality. This provides a totally new perspective but also an entirely different responsibility and many more opportunities. Only then can life become real. If you acknowledge your own Divine nature and creative power you will be able to recognise the unification with us, the spiritual world, in your heart. Unifying with us is an act of love. It is a connection of the heart that is available to everybody because we are nothing other than a part of every person's heart. The Christ-energy is part of everyone's heart. By making contact with us you make contact with a very intimate part of yourself. To realise this contact we suggest you pray."

"But what is a prayer? Let us start at the beginning. A prayer is a way of making a connection between yourself and an unconditional source of love. By praying to this source of love you bring this source to yourself and thus activate your own unconditional source of love from inside. The two sources can resonate with each other. You can experience the unity of these two sources on a subtle level. They are one."

"The unconditional source of love that you invoke through prayer can also be epitomised by powers or energies that represent a specific aspect of this source. We – Mary, Jesus and Mary Magdalene – are examples of these powers along with other spiritual masters of the White Brother- and Sisterhood, such as Buddha, Maitreya, Jacob and Joseph who all have a subservient task with respect to this world."

"You have a certain amount of free will, which enables you to make certain choices. You can decide between all sorts of experiences. You can create various realities for yourself. And occasionally, pain and stress can present themselves within the realities you wish to experience. We may not interfere in this. Only when you invoke us by means of prayer may we help and support you in solving conflicts and finding the way to your heart. Through prayer you open up a door, as it were, to unconditional love in your own consciousness. You take a step from your pseudo-identity to your true self! You take a step towards a consciousness of unity. This is the quickest way to allow love into your life!"

"Some people have an aversion to praying. They think they must and can do everything on their own. They haughtily close themselves off in loneliness and pain, thus needlessly prolonging the 'process of agony'. Actually, they are afraid of love. They suffered a disappointment once and became wary and now no longer dare to trust. Deep down they long for love, but they are afraid of it. This fear is often concealed under a coating of arrogance, 'Oh, I can do it all myself.' If you belong to this group of people, there are two things you can do:

- Wait until someday a crisis in your life or approaching death brings you to prayer.
- Give prayer a chance now and experience it several times, objectively. And let it influence your own life."

"Some people have had bad experiences with certain official religious institutions that have claimed all rights to prayer. These institutions have been an attempt, in the history of mankind, to protect certain spiritual traditions. They fulfil a need for many people and that is fine. But in principle you do not need them to experience a direct connection with the source of love. No go-betweens are needed between you and God. There is a direct link. Our advice is: 'Try again and make direct connect. We are waiting for you'."

Prayer to a higher source of love

"If you feel inhibited due to unpleasant experiences in the past, you can also pray to be allowed to divest yourself of them. When you pray you are prepared to surrender yourself to a greater awareness of love, making all the cells in the body and all the different levels of energy in man resonate on a higher frequency. You are elevated into an awareness of love. Enjoy it. You may pray for anything – for very important matters in life as well as for small things. The more you pray the easier your life becomes and the happier you will feel."

"What kind of prayer can you use? Basically, any prayer that is addressed to a higher source of love. You can pray directly to God.

You can address yourself to a spiritual master. You can also make your own prayer from the heart. You can also pray to us – Mary, Jesus and Mary Magdalene. And for this purpose we wish to share some prayers with you that have a high energy frequency and a special power."

Prayer to God

*Almighty God
I ask you
In the name of Jesus Christ your son
Have mercy upon me
Amen*

"Say this several times and let it register. You can also request something else you may need. And this could be anything. You can make your request at the end of the prayer, as follows:"

Have mercy upon me and help me with ....

Prayer to Jesus Christ

"You can also pray directly to Jesus Christ."

*Lord Jesus Christ
Son of God
Have mercy upon me
Amen*

Jesus: "Let this prayer register as well. And know that I, Jesus, love you; that I descended onto Earth to share love with you. That we are one together. I did not visit Earth to accuse you or to declare you sinful or imperfect. I came to remind you that love is the power of the universe to unify and that you have that power within you as well."

"Being the 'Son of God' is a manifestation of the creative power of God, i.e., the given shape of the will of God. All that exists is Divine and created by God. Everyone is actually a son or daughter of God. Every person is in an awareness process to realise that he or she is God. Realise that you are a child (a creation) of God and at the same time you are God yourself. You have created yourself. You yourself are the trinity: the Father (the creator), the Son (the creation) and the Holy Spirit (the creative power)."

"You and I are one and the same. When you are afraid of me, when you have an aversion towards me and when you feel guilty or accused, we lose each other. And then we too – the spiritual masters – lose the essence of our existence. It is perfectly alright to approach me and awaken the source of love within yourself. Then our mission on Earth will be fulfilled. We journey together to our own essence, yours and mine, for they are the same. But first some more prayers; for these, I would like first of all to call upon my beloved Mary Magdalene."

Prayer to Mary Magdalene

Mary Magdalene: "Dear brothers and sisters, I have come a long way to reach you. But here I am, a Divine woman. The world is ready for me now. And the world needs me to come into balance, to heal. What is one half without the other? Like a table with only half its legs that loses its balance and topples over. And that is what has happened to the world. By denying me for the past two thousand years, the world has become very much unbalanced. Look around you, and look within yourself and you will notice it. You have come far in your consciousness to be ready for me, to be able to accept the female principle; this is why I have come. Look at me with respect and admiration. Open your heart of love to me, allow me into your life. I bring warmth into the heart, equilibrium and harmony between the masculine and the feminine. Both men and women can summon my energy by means of the following prayer."

Dear Mary Magdalene
Divine woman
Have mercy upon me and awaken in me
Help me to heal and appreciate the female principle within me
In all the depths of my being, in my fellow man and in everything
on Earth
Amen

"Let this prayer register. We will discuss the communication to and fro between the male and female principles and its greater significance elsewhere in this book (see Revelations 11 and 12). But first I now call upon my mother, Mary, to speak."

Prayer to Mary

Mary: "Dear children, I have come to take you onto my lap. To ease your sorrow and worries. To awaken the flame in your heart. I am the female and motherly principle. I am the Divine mother from which all is created. I am the holy womb that gives birth and brings life to all. In this womb I also bear you, so that you can feel you are perfect and recognise and acknowledge yourself as such. It is completely alright to call upon me at any time in your life. My love is infinite and you may drink it in. Invoke me in your heart and I will be there because I am actually always there. By invoking me you will become aware of this. You can appeal to me in the following way."

Dear Mary
Divine mother of Heaven and Earth
Have mercy upon me
Awaken the love in my heart for all that exists and for myself
Help me to live with an open mind like a Divine child
That is amazed about everything
And that treats everything in this Heavenly paradise with love
and respect
Help me to let my Divine essence awaken completely

To be who I actually am in Heaven and on Earth
And that your love and my love, dear Mother, may be one
For now and forever
Amen

"Let this prayer resound within you. It can heal everything within you at all levels. You have many unnecessary tensions, fears and worries in your life. It is now time to let them go. Surrender them to us. Let yourself be supported by us. This prayer will help you to do so. It is advisable to learn the Prayer to Mary by heart and to say it to yourself several times a day. The Prayer to Mary contains all the aspects required to make a connection with the Divine world. We will now look at the various parts of the Prayer in more detail."

'Dear Mary, Divine mother of Heaven and Earth'

"This first sentence makes it clear that the energy of Mary is present all over the universe and that it is an essential and inextricable part of all that exists. It is the energy of the Heavenly mother that is present in Divine powers and therefore also in you."

'Have mercy upon me'

"With this you request the power of Mary to connect with you. You become aware of the connection that in fact already exists. The energy of Mary is already present in everyone's heart. By saying the prayer you make the connection that activates this energy."

'Awaken the love in my heart for all that exists and for myself'
"Only if your hearts open up and you love yourself unconditionally can you love others. Then there is true love. Until that time you can only look for yourself in others. And then you will never find yourself. Only if you grant yourself love and give yourself the attention that you like to seek so often in others will you create the basis for love in life. A love that you can later share with others."

'Help me to live with an open mind like a Divine child that is amazed about everything'

"The feeling that you 'need nothing' to feel valuable is the basis of the love for yourself. That feeling comes by embracing and accepting, unconditionally and without criticism, the welcome and less welcome aspects in your heart with love. If you have that feeling, you need no acceptance from others to feel peace in your heart. You are OK! There is nothing wrong with you, and you know it. That is the basis for the safe feeling of 'being open-minded'. It is a childlike feeling. Being open-minded creates room for amazement. Amazement about others, amazement about the world in all its beauty and Divinity. Experience them with joy and take pleasure in them!"

'And that treats everything in this Heavenly paradise with love and respect'

"Amazement is another word for love and respect. Connection is love, appreciation is respect. True love and respect can develop only from an open-minded heart with no hidden agendas."
'Help me to let my Divine essence awaken completely,
To be who I actually am in Heaven and on Earth'

"You are Divine beings. Becoming aware of this brings you in touch with your true self, both in heavenly form (consciousness) and in earthly form (incarnation). Together they are an entity."

'And that your love and my love, dear Mother, may be one'

"If you are in contact with Mary in your heart, you experience bliss and compassion. Compassion is pure love and acceptance. The awakening of Mary in your own heart is the awakening of compassion in yourself. You and I, Mary, are one. Then our love is one."

'For now and forever'

"From the third dimension of time and space, via the way of compassion, you proceed to the fourth dimension beyond space and time. And then on to the fifth dimension of unconditional love."

'Amen'

"With this you state your intention and call up universal powers of love that help you realise your prayer."

(The prayers are repeated in larger print in a separate chapter at the back of this book)

Revelation 5

Mary requests people's attention for the victim/offender consciousness and makes suggestions as to transformation. She makes herself available as a representative of compassion and as a spiritual guide in the individual transformation process whenever people pray for this. Exercise with respect to man's relationship with his or her personal ambitions and the impact of ambitions on everyone's lives.

Mary: "I came onto Earth to relieve your suffering. I am the representative of compassion. An important task at this time is to transform the human victim/offender consciousness. The crucial transformation in human consciousness consists of resolving the dichotomy that every person carries within, namely the ostensible dichotomy between the material human apparition on Earth and the Divine nature of man in the spiritual world. This transformation can be activated by accepting and working out your patterns of thought that impede you in the elimination of this false antithesis. Growing insight into the victim/offender relationship leads to the most significant change in your consciousness that you must undergo in order to become aware of your Divine essence even as an incarnated human being on Earth."

"But not everyone is ready for this. Some people have not yet completely worked out the experience of being the victim or the offender. They still feel that they are the victim of certain situations or people. They do not want to bear responsibility for what they have created in their own lives, do not want to acknowledge their own part in it. Furthermore, they often do not understand what their responsibility is in this respect. Only when they open themselves up in order to understand their responsibility and pray for it, for instance, can they become aware of their responsibility and free themselves from the illusion of being a victim by no longer pointing the finger at the others, the offenders, but by examining and being keenly sensible to their own part in their situations in life. Every person who feels that he or she is usually a victim or an offender in this life is totally trapped in this experience. Both the so-called victim and the so-called offender are, however, completely equally matched and stage an act together. The acknowledgement and acceptance of this as well as the forgiveness and deep understanding this entails contribute significantly to opening the heart.

An important aspect of understanding the victim/offender experience is realising that you are or have been both a victim and an offender. In most cases, if at one time you started a certain life in one role, you will also want to experience the other role in order to fathom and complete your experience of this ostensible dichotomy. These kinds of processes are worked out all the time on Earth. This can only stop when you are prepared to accept your responsibility for the event and when you have the courage to look at both sides of the experience and forgive yourself and the other."

"Incidentally, doing away with the victim/offender consciousness is one of the greatest capitulations of the ego. This is why people hold onto the pattern so tightly. Taking responsibility for one's spiritual growth is the key to higher knowledge and insight. It is also the most important aspect for opening the heart. For those who are not yet ready to transform this pattern on their own, I – Mary – am the right person to whom you can turn for support and relief. Although I am prepared to comfort you and take you by the hand in all the steps needed to arrive at a transformation, I am not prepared to confirm you in your role of victim/offender. My presence remains an example and a reflection of the light within you. And by being in contact with me, sooner or later you will come into contact with your own inner light. Confirming you in the victim/offender role would be equal to denying someone's light and this can lead to severe spiritual damage."

Mary supports transformation

"There have been extraterrestrial entities who promoted the victim/offender consciousness on Earth. This is now so firmly anchored in the consciousness on Earth that it is still the most dominant pattern in human consciousness today. Victims, offenders and saviours are the most active archetypes in the media, in politics and in personal, human relations. Yet, since the 1960s, there is a growing process on Earth in which, to an ever greater extent, you take your own responsibility for your own life and for the whole. We also see more and more indications in the media and in available knowledge from which you can draw inspiration and support."

"You also tend to blame the spiritual world for what you have created yourself, such as the events in your own lives. By doing so, you block a positive and supportive connection with the spiritual world. We are not offended and do not react to your interpretations. We observe this with compassion and love and accept it as a part of your process. This attitude only has negative and painful consequences for you yourselves. It is a downward spiral that draws you further away from your own light. By feeling a victim, you wait to be saved by the spiritual world or by God and become angry when this does not happen. You have forgotten the most important purpose of being on Earth, namely to develop your own spiritual powers and consciousness, to become aware of your own Divine nature; every little step counts."

"Your ego often calls for high ambitions and when these ambitions are not realised you consider yourself to have failed. Then you blame God or the White Brother- and Sisterhood and feel you are a victim. However, when you look at your own capacities attentively and with respect, you can create a life that fits you and you need not feel that you are a victim. Our love and our light can then resonate with you and your heart will open up. You can then continue to grow. If you are prepared to look at yourself from this perspective, you will open the door to love in this life. And that counts for everyone, even if you are already engaged in this process. When, deep in your heart, you have already taken the decision to let go of these old mental patterns and stand in your own power, you can call on us – Mary and the other spiritual guides – through prayer to support your process (see Revelation 4). You can come to us with all your questions and worries. Of course, if you have not yet taken this decision, you can contact us anyway, also through prayer, and we will give you as much light as you are prepared to accept."

Exercise – Becoming aware of the influence of ambitions

"This exercise provides insight into where you stand in relation to your ambitions and the impact of ambitions on your life. Do your ambitions reflect your heart or your ego? Which need are you trying to fulfil with your ambition? Is this realistic? Contemplating your ambitions can have a liberating effect on your life."

• Draw up a list of your main ambitions.

• Next to each ambition, list the underlying need that you wish to fulfil by realising the ambition.

• Recognise the need for the first ambition on your list and embrace it with love in your heart.

• Do you expect recognition from others upon realising this ambition? Give yourself the recognition you wish for from others.

• Breathe into the belly and feel what it is like to get this recognition.

• Enjoy it and continue on to your next ambition.

• Repeat the exercise for all the ambitions on your list and continue to apply it to each new ambition you add to your list.

Revelation 6

Mary, Jesus and Mary Magdalene draw people's attention to the fact that they should lead a life of awareness. They compare giving life content with maintaining a garden. Modern man has little thought for the inner self. People's ability to penetrate their inner self in order to make contact with the spiritual aspect of themselves is an essential part of life. Exercise to become aware of shifting attention and its effects.

Mary, Jesus and Mary Magdalene: "Life is like a garden. In a garden, each plant should have its own space. The garden gets its beauty from its order and colours, but mainly from each plant and each stone being positioned in the right place. This can be compared with a person's life in which all aspects of life – physical, emotional, mental and spiritual – must have their own space. Due to the pressure and struggle in current society, many of you are not motivated to pay attention to these essential aspects. You are busy trying to fulfil all your needs and ambitions. And you forget to pay attention to the harmony in your own garden, in your own inner self. Your inner garden is often chaotic. Weeds abound, the plants are untended and there are leaves all over the place. You have little time to sit in your garden. By looking at your 'inner garden' you become agitated and do not get enough input to be able to create harmony. If we project this metaphor onto society, then society becomes restless too. This creates a vicious circle, making you feel unsafe in society with the result that you become even more disquieted."

Foster tranquillity again

"You can break through this vicious circle by fostering the connection with your inner self once more. Penetrating yourself to make contact with the spiritual is an essential part of life. It is the basis on which you can continue to build. To make contact with your inner self you need to shift your attention from the outside to within and foster the tranquillity within yourself. One way to do this is to start and end the day with prayer. And it is also good to pray again sometime in-between during the day. Through prayer, you are connected directly with a higher level of consciousness and a higher level of love. In this way you will remember your own Divine essence, and that is really what you are unconsciously seeking. The fulfilment that you expect to obtain from your outward life will ultimately be found in once again consciously experiencing your own Divine essence. We realise that you also have a need at this time to occupy yourself purposefully with creating on Earth, in order to shape your own life. You are the creators of your own reality by the decisions you make, by how you shape your life, by the way in which you deal with relationships, studies, work, dwelling, etc., etc. After you have created this life of your own, you forget that you yourself have brought it about and then you often feel at variance with the circumstances you created yourself. You feel you are victims, whereas actually you are creators."

"The souls that are currently incarnated on Earth have a need to experience the current manifestation of matter on Earth. To feel like a creator in this. Your greatest challenge is to experience the unity between 'outside' and 'inside'. You may ask our help for this at any time."

Exercise – Experiencing shifting your awareness

"The purpose of the following exercise is for you to experience shifting your awareness from outside to inside and vice versa, as well as its effects. Varying both experiences will integrate them and bring you tranquillity and freedom.

• Withdraw to a quiet place.

• Close your eyes and focus your attention on your breathing.

• Breathe deeply into the belly and feel how you relax.

• Shift your attention to all the aspects in your life with which you are occupied every day. Explore them one by one, slowly and objectively.

• Become aware of the reactions that each aspect of your life arouses in you and accept these reactions.

• What do you seek in all these daily activities?

• Feel what your innermost wishes are and accept them.

• Now shift your attention to your heart.

• Make contact with the unconditional love that is in your heart.

• Breathe deeply into the belly and feel how this love feels.

• Make contact with the calm that is in your heart.

• Breathe deeply into the belly and feel how this calm feels.

• Make contact with the submission that is in your heart.

• Breathe deeply into the belly and feel how this submission feels.

• Make contact with the fulfilment that is in your heart.

• Breathe deeply into the belly and feel how this fulfilment feels.

• Shift your attention back to all the aspects of your life with which you are occupied every day. Explore them again, slowly, one by one and objectively.

• Become aware of the reactions that each aspect of your life arouses in you and accept these reactions.

• What do you seek in all these daily activities?

• Feel what your innermost wishes are and accept them.

• Now shift your attention to your heart.

• Make contact with the unconditional love that is in your heart.

• Breathe deeply into the belly and feel how this love feels.

• Make contact with the calm that is in your heart.

• Breathe deeply into the belly and feel how this calm feels.

• Make contact with the submission that is in your heart.

• Breathe deeply into the belly and feel how this submission feels.

• Make contact with the fulfilment that is in your heart.

• Breathe deeply into the belly and feel how this fulfilment feels.

• Continue to shift your attention from inside to outside and back until you experience tranquillity deep within.

• Enjoy it and give yourself all the time you need to experience it.

• Open your eyes and return to the here and now."

Revelation 7

Mary, Jesus and Mary Magdalene draw man's attention to the five development stages in becoming aware of one's inner self. Exercises to help one recognise one's own stage of development.

Mary, Jesus and Mary Magdalene: "Perhaps you have noticed that you are trained in society to play parts. This is a Divine play. Just think of the roles of father, mother, child, employee, employer, artist or beggar. Or you foster capacities or limitations on the order of 'I am intelligent, beautiful, worthwhile' or 'I don't count, I'm stupid, they're always out to get me', etc. Since childhood, you are prepared and trained to be able to meet certain expectations. You are programmed to assume certain roles under various circumstances. Nevertheless, you try to be as much yourself and as authentic as possible in the various roles that you play. You barely succeed in this because you often lose yourself in your assumed role, you identify too strongly with it, so that you no longer realise it is only a role. The result is that people often function at two levels, namely that of outward appearance and that of the inner self."

"We would now like to discuss the level of the inner self, that which is actually inside you. What is the essence of being here on Earth for every individual? Actually, we are all spiritual explorers. Everyone has his or her own quest and a clear reason for being here on Earth. So you have different kinds of connections with your inner process. Some of you are connected subconsciously with your inner self. Others are slightly more aware, but are still hesitant to trust this connection. Others trust it every once in a while and then again they do not. Another group completely trusts the call of their own heart, of their inner process, and bases their outward life on it. They have integrated their inner life and their outward manifestation in everyday life to a considerable extent. A somewhat smaller group follows their own heart completely and shares it with others."

"A growth process is required to progress from the first to the fifth stage. The same applies to everyone: try to feel in which stage of development you are. You can ask yourself whether you want to be inspired in this process. If the answer is 'yes', the following is important for you. By recognising in which stage you are you can take a more conscious view of yourself. This book inspires you along on this path. The following is a brief description of what it feels like in each of these different stages."

Stage 1

"You are not aware of your quest on Earth and you have the feeling that something is missing, that there is something very essential but that it eludes you. You feel a kind of emptiness in yourself. The fulfilment you get out of external matters is only temporary. You feel an underlying sorrow. This feeling of emptiness and sorrow brings you to stage 2."

Stage 2

"In this stage you have become aware that there is more than the outward life. But it feels very confrontational to listen to the voice of your heart. You have the feeling that if you would really listen to this voice it would cause changes in your outward life and you are not up to that yet. A certain kind of tension is created between knowing and not wanting to know. This tension brings you to stage 3."

Stage 3

"You can no longer deny the voice of your own heart and you start to become aware of the sorrow and the empty feeling that this denial entails. You decide to try it and then occasionally follow the voice of your heart. This gives fulfilment, but the confrontation with those aspects of your life in which you do not follow your heart becomes increasingly stronger. The purity of your heart begins to penetrate into your life. This brings you to stage 4."

Stage 4

"You have become aware of the fact that the voice of your heart is the only true source. You surrender to a life from the heart with all its consequences. This is a phase of transformation. Submission and trust are the essential concepts in this stage. You begin to discover the essence of life. This level gives access to higher states of consciousness. It is a natural development that brings you to stage 5."

Stage 5

"This is the level of brother- and sisterhood. You want to share what you discover with others. You want to inspire others to listen to their own heart. You realise that your own process also mirrors other people's processes. You become more open in order to be able to connect yourself on a collective level as well. Sharing the process of your own heart is then a way towards unity."

"Would you like to examine your own situation? Then do the following short exercises.

The Divinity of Mankind

Exercise – In which stage of awareness development am I?

• Study the five stages and recognise in which stage of development you are at this point in time.

• Feel what it feels like to be in this stage.

• Accept this feeling.

Exercise – What is the innermost desire of my heart?

• Listen to your heart.

• Breathe deeply into the belly and feel what the innermost desire of your heart is.

• Open yourself to achieve this desire in your life.

• Enjoy this opportunity."

Revelation 8

Mary Magdalene presents herself from the spiritual world and tells what Jesus and Mary mean to her and what the reasons are for the publication of this book. Mary Magdalene explains what God is and provides the 'I am God' exercises and a prayer to let people experience their Divine essence and accept it into their heart.

Mary Magdalene: "I have come to heal the female energy on Earth, to show what the essence of the female is and what the essence is of all the possibilities that a woman has within her. I have come to do better justice to all the subtle elements that are present in every woman on Earth. The same applies to the female aspect in every man, which must be brought into balance with his male energy."

"My dearly beloved Jesus is on my right and on my left is my dearest Mary, my spiritual mother, the mother of my heart who supports me with all her love. Jesus is my beloved without whom I would not be who I am today. They support me and they let me 'be born'. Together we are a trinity that is of service to you."

"I invite you all to pore over our Revelations in order to sample their essence and make yourself familiar with them. To awaken the essence within yourself. We are a mirror of your own Divinity. We have come here to remind you of this fact. This is also symbolised in Jesus' words during the healing of Lazarus when Jesus says: 'Arise and walk!' You can also arise now and be who you really are. Namely to live on this Earth based on your Divine essence."

What is God?

"You have often tended to project all sorts of images onto God with which you felt comfortable, such as 'God as an old man with a beard'. You also associated existential dilemmas with God: 'How can God let this terrible thing happen.' The images that many of you have used were aimed at placing God outside yourself and thus not having to take any responsibility for your own Divinity. Many keep God at a distance. How else can one interpret, for example: 'God as father in Heaven' or 'God as a punishing father'."

"However, the infinite dimension of God can hardly be grasped by the human mind. That doesn't matter. In this connection I would like to advise you to approach God with an open mind and free of any prejudice, so that the Divine can unfold and manifest itself in you to an even greater extent. Because God is in everybody's heart and consciousness, you yourself are God. From that perspective you might consider sometime how you use your own creative power. What is your own role in all sorts of Earthly events, large and small? It is important in this connection to realise that you are much more than the human consciousness. The higher levels of consciousness on which you take certain decisions will only be revealed when you are prepared to view yourself from this perspective and when you open your heart. Not taking responsibility for your own deeds, passivity and creations and laying all the 'blame' on God is outdated on Earth."

"God is much more than can be described with words. Still, here is an attempt, an indication. God is everything. God is love and compassion. God is humour and sorrow. God is matter and consciousness. God is past, present and future. God is meaningless and full of meaning. God is. God is the being of everything that exists. God is all human races. God is all religions. God comprises all levels of consciousness. God is holistic. People are a manifestation of God, you are God. Each molecule in the universe reflects the whole. There is nothing that is not a part of God. The idea, for instance, that there could be a dichotomy between God and the devil is a projection of the human mind. The dichotomy between God and the devil is only a projection of your own duality, your view on good and evil. God is everything and is above all duality. What you consider to be the devil is in fact nothing other than your own fear of your undesirable aspects. At an absolute level there is no duality. All is one, all is God, you too. Even experiences that in the eyes of man could in no way be part of God, actually are. From your Earthly point of view, you cannot always understand the deeper purpose of the Divine plan. Many apparently terrible events are in essence an expression of love and compassion. In order to be able to experience and understand it as such your consciousness must be in a further stage of development. In this respect, it is especially important that you also have the courage to accept your so-called undesirable aspects and all your so-called imperfections, which are also Divine, and to integrate them into your being in order to become more sincere towards yourself and more authentic."

Three essences

"However, acknowledging your being God also entails responsibility. Everything that exists in the universe is God. You are not the only one who is Divine. This is good news. There is equality. In your manifestation on Earth you must be aware and remain aware of everything around you, of plants, animals, people, of Mother Earth and of all the stars and planets in the universe. You are an entity. Make sure that you behave on this Earth with respect and love towards them. Take pleasure from them. Admire them. So that you can admire yourself. Experience the unity. And let the feeling of unity flow through you."

"The first essence I mentioned in this respect is: "I am God', the second essence is: 'The world is God' and the third essence is: 'We are one!'. We will discuss the latter two essences in subsequent Revelations. The following are several exercises to help you become aware of the first essence.

Exercise 1 – I am God

"Your essence is love, your essence lives in your heart. Love is also your power. Yet you do not live much from the heart in the here and now. You can make loving connections with your surroundings, with people in your life, with people in the street, but mainly with yourself. Who of you can say: 'From my heart: 'I love myself'.' You often tend to condemn yourself and others. This ultimately leads to fears, loneliness and sorrow. The answer to 'Who am I really?' is:

'I am God'

- Feel this in your heart. Close your eyes and repeat to yourself: 'I am God'. Let it register. Let it flow inward from your heart like nectar.

- Let this joyful message flow through to each cell. The message is then passed on to each cell to remind it to wake up again. And each cell feels: 'I am God!'.

This message brings happiness, responsibility and humility. Life is easy. You are OK, complete in yourself! There is nothing missing. Isn't that good news?! You don't have to do anything. You need not put much effort into it or strive to correct your alleged imperfections. You no longer need to prove that you are 'good'. The idea of being no good does not exist in the Divine world. Everything is in perfect harmony. You came to this world to play, to experience, to feel what it is like to be a part of God in matter. To manifest yourself as you are. Acknowledging this brings bliss and tranquillity. Enjoy yourself. Explore yourself. Admire yourself. You can do the following exercise to strengthen your insight as to 'I am God'.

- Find a quiet place and withdraw there.

- Close your eyes and let your breathing quiet down.

- Repeat intently in your heart 'I am God'.

- Breathe into the belly and feel what is happening to your body.

- Make a connection between your heart and your physical feeling.

- Give yourself time to experience this.

- Again repeat intently in your heart "I am God".

- Breathe into the belly and feel what is happening to your emotions.

- Make a connection between your heart and your emotions.

- Give yourself time to experience this.

- Again repeat intently in your heart "I am God".

- Breathe deeply into the belly and feel what is happening to your thoughts.

- Make a connection between your heart and your thoughts.

- Give yourself time to experience this.

- Open yourself to this.

- Feel whether there is any resistance to accepting that you are God. Feel each resistance and just let it be.

- Make a connection between your heart and your resistance.

- Bring your resistance into the light and let it go.

- Bring your attention back to your heart.

- Experience the tranquillity in your heart.

• Feel every recognition as well.

• Receive every recognition in your heart.

• Accept every feeling. Become aware of it.

• When you are ready, open your eyes and return to the here and now.

You have often denied your own divine nature during your evolutionary process. You have repeated this message of denial many times to every cell, resulting in confusion and denial of your true identity. This ignorance and this denial cover your consciousness and your body like a blanket of fog. A layer of fog lies over every cell. Acknowledging that 'I am God' will lift the fog.

• Repeat this exercise often and feel what it does to you. Let the fog lift.

I am with you to support you. You may say my name, Mary Magdalene, in your heart at the start, during and at the end of this exercise in support of your process. Later, you can make a drawing or a description of yourself in which you describe your experiences during this exercise in expressive and precise terms.

Exercise 2 – Connection between heart and name

• Close your eyes and let your breathing calm down.

• Repeat your own name, your first and last names, what you call yourself.

• Breathe into the belly and feel how that feels.

• Make an instinctive connection between your heart and your name.

• Accept everything that you feel.

• Connect each feeling with your heart.

• Breathe into the belly and feel every sensation.

• Give yourself time to experience this.

• Open your eyes and return to the here and now.

Exercise 3 – I am God

• Select a number of photographs of several valuable moments in your life, from when you were a baby up to the present. Pictures of you alone.

• Project yourself into who you were then.

• With your eyes closed, repeat to yourself: 'I am God'.

• Breathe into the belly and feel what is happening to you.

• Let every feeling and every thought into your heart. Take enough time to experience in this way every phase in your life that comes into your mind.

• Become aware of the different stages of life. Was there a time that you still knew within yourself that you were God? Did you forget this at some stage? Or did you start denying it?

• Keep a diary of what you experience through these four exercises. Preferably in a binder with loose pages so that you can shred them once you have completed a certain phase."

Prayer

"In closing I am giving you a prayer to let your awareness of 'being God' awaken in your heart."

Dear God
Mother and Father God
All-embracing power that is in my heart
Awaken in me
And help me so that I at all times in my life
In every word, with every deed and act
Will be aware of my Divinity
Help me to manifest the Divine love on Earth
And with me in every fellow man
Amen

Revelation 9

Mary provides exercises for man to experience the Divine in the world. The main cause of pain in people is the insufficient extent to which they experience the Divine in themselves and in the world. It is mainly thoughts, opinions and convictions that block out the Divine. To experience God in the world, mankind must let go of its old assumptions and revere the world.

Mary: "The second exercise, following on Revelation 8, deals with the next essence, namely 'The world is God'. Being able to perceive God in the external world, in one's fellow man, in the plants, the animals, nature, the stars. Experiencing the Divine nature of all that exists. The Divine can show itself in you and in the world. You do not consciously experience the Divine in yourself and in the world, which is the main cause of the inner pain many of you suffer. How can I consciously experience God in the world? How can I experience God in my fellow man, in my partner, in our child, in my neighbour? How can I experience God in my cat or in my dog? Can I experience God in nature? The following exercises will help you answer these questions."

Exercise 1 – Step 1: Becoming aware of the attention in your mind

"Prepare yourself for a trip. We are going on a trip to experience God in the world. To experience God in the world you must let go of your convictions. They stand between you and God. We will do a short three-step exercise to experience this letting go.

- Withdraw to a quiet place where you cannot be disturbed. Make yourself comfortable in a chair.

- Play soft meditative music, close your eyes and make contact with your breathing.

- Breathe deeply into the belly and feel how you relax.

- Become aware of all your thoughts, opinions, convictions, ideas, the things you still have to do, everything that requires attention.

- Turn your attention back to yourself, to your breathing and feel how you relax.

- Realise: I can control my attention, I decide what my attention is focused on.

- Become aware of what your attention is turning to and ask yourself whether this is a deliberate choice.

- Then let your attention turn to each thought or conviction that announces itself, experience it for a moment and then turn your attention back to yourself, back to your breathing. Do this several times.

- What do you feel? Make a note of this for yourself.

Exercise 1 – Step 2: Becoming aware of the attention in your heart

- Keep your attention focused on yourself.

- Breathe deeply into the belly and feel how you relax.

- Abandon all ideas and thoughts.

- If your attention turns to your thoughts, calmly turn it back to your heart

- Feel what is happening to you. Focus completely on every part of yourself that demands attention.

- Breathe deeply into the belly and feel how that feels.

- Explore yourself. Become aware of yourself.

- Completely accept the way you are.

- Repeat to yourself 'I am OK'.

- Feel how it feels to say that.

- Admire yourself.

Exercise 1 - Step 3: Observing from the heart

- Play calm meditative music. Let the music in with total receptivity.

- Breathe deeply into the belly and feel how you relax.

- You do not have to react to anything. You do not have to have an opinion on the music. Just let it in and experience it. How does it feel? How does it feel in your heart?

- Accept the music as it is.

- Admire the music.

- Breathe deeply into the belly and feel how that feels.

- Repeat this exercise several times.

• If the exercise feels liberating, you can replace the music by an image, a feeling or a scent. Everything can be experienced with total acceptance. Note down your experiences to help you follow the process better.

You can do this exercise everywhere. The purpose of the exercise is to recognise where your attention is: in your head or in your heart? The attention in your head projects your own thoughts onto the external world, as a result of which your perception of the external world is coloured. All you are doing is looking at your own interpretation of yourself and of the world, your own inner movie. You cannot perceive the world and everything that is part of the world as it really is from your head. You can only see your own interpretation of the world. However, when your attention is in your heart, you calm down and you can let the world in, into your own heart. Then you can focus your full attention on an object in the world and accept the object for what it is. In this way you can experience the Divine in the world. A good way to do this is to go for a walk and then detect the movement of your attention from your head to your heart. You are then moving back and forth between your interpretation on the one hand and a feeling of emptiness and susceptibility on the other hand. Experience the difference between what happens when your attention is in your head or in your heart. Let this experience influence your choice: do I want to be in my heart or in my head? You are now able to decide what you want to do with your attention. It is up to you."

Revelation 10

Man longs most for unity. Thoughts, convictions and opinions create an involuntary illusion about the world and about ourselves. Jesus gives exercises to eliminate man's feeling of being cut off from the rest of the world. "Love is the connective force that makes us aware of the unity between ourselves and the world."

Jesus: "The third essence mentioned in Revelation 8 was 'We are one'. I would therefore like to discuss man's great longing. What is it you long for? There is only one thing you really long for and that is *unity*! Unity already exists but how can you feel it? How can you solve the feeling of being divided from the rest of the world? What is dividing you? It is only your thoughts, convictions and opinions that divide you. They create an unconscious interpretation of the world and of yourself. And you share that interpretation, along with its various aspects, with everyone on Earth, thus creating a collective illusion. You fuel this collective illusion continually and this keeps mankind in a kind of collective trance, in a kind of hypnosis. It is now possible to 'reawaken'. However, the masses of thoughts, opinions and convictions you have created still envelop the world like a thick blanket of fog. Besides the individual assumptions, these masses are fuelled extensively by the media and by various forces in the world, such as political, social, financial and religious systems. The step required to awaken and to lift the fog is simple. We, the White Brother- and Sisterhood, would like to guide you on this journey. Not much is required to let the fog vanish. Only one thing is crucial and that is the intention from the heart to do it. The intention to love yourself and the world, the intention to recognise and experience the unity. We provide two tools: exercises and prayers. Both means support each other.

Exercises to awaken the consciousness of unity

"The following exercises are aimed at awakening the consciousness of unity between you and the world. The Divinity in yourself and the Divinity in the world are essentially one big field of consciousness, one Divine entity, of which love is the essence.

Love Exercise 1

• Make yourself comfortable in a chair and close your eyes.

• Breathe deeply into the belly and feel how you relax.

• Turn your attention back to yourself and observe yourself.

• Observe your own body, from head to toe.

• Feel your emotions and sensations. And allow them to be. Accept everything in yourself. You do not have to change a thing. Give yourself time to experience this.

• Continue until you feel love flow from your heart throughout your body.

Love Exercise 2

• Focus on a person, animal, plant or object that is precious to you.

• Accept him, her or it completely.

• Turn your attention to your heart and close an imaginary love contract between your heart and this person, this animal, this plant or this object until you clearly experience a connection.

• Continue until you feel love flow from your heart to whom or what you are focusing on.

• Repeat Love Exercises 1 and 2 up to this point until you feel a loving unity between yourself and whom or what you are focusing on.

• Do this exercise as often as possible in all sorts of circumstances and with all sorts of people, animals, plants and objects, even the least precious.

Love Exercise 3

Once you have had some practice you can do this exercise with your eyes open. By repeating the exercise more often you will create a connective force that leads to a consciousness of unity. This connective force is known as love. Love is the connective force that makes us aware of the unity between ourselves and the world."

Revelation 11

Mary about Mary as a symbol of mother, wife and sister, about the essence of woman and man and the true nature of their interaction, about her relationship with Joseph as an example for mankind. About the true meaning of the 'Immaculate Conception' and the role of the Holy Spirit. To conceive Jesus, Mary and Joseph did indeed have physical contact.

Mary: "I would now like to discuss the female principle. I ask both women and men to be open-minded and unprejudiced in this respect. Before reading further, I recommend you say the prayers to Mary Magdalene and me (Mary) several times and let them sink in. This will prepare you."

Dear Mary Magdalene
Divine woman
Have mercy upon me and awaken in me
Help me to heal and appreciate the female principle within me
In all the depths of my being, in my fellow man and in everything
on Earth
Amen

Dear Mary
Divine mother of Heaven and Earth
Have mercy upon me
Awaken the love in my heart for all that exists and for myself
Help me to live with an open mind like a Divine child
That is amazed about everything
And that treats everything in this Heavenly paradise with love
and respect

Help me to let my Divine essence awaken completely
To be who I actually am in Heaven and on Earth
And that your love and my love, dear mother, may be one
For now and forever
Amen

Mary: mother, wife and sister

"During the past two thousand years a thick blanket of fog has been placed, as it were, over Jesus' partner, the Divine woman Mary Magdalene. And with her over all women in the world. I am the only woman who represents the female principle, who has really been allowed to be. You see in me the maternal aspect, while you do not look upon me as the wife or partner of a man. The Bible wrongly divides the three aspects of the female principle into Mary the mother, Mary the wife and Mary as a sister. These three principles are all an intrinsic part of each woman, even if she has no children, has no partner and has no brothers or sisters in her family. The three principles nourish each other and need each other. All three are unconditional and altruistic."

"The woman in all her aspects is usually a mystery to the man. A man can only discover a woman and connect with her if he lives from the heart and approaches her with respect and love. If a man does not live from the heart, he often feels powerless to discover her and to really commit himself to her. If he feels powerless, he often projects his own frustrations onto her. She is no good in his view and that makes him rebel. Instead of withdrawing into his heart, he attacks her and rejects her. He blames her for his unhappiness. And then it becomes increasingly more complex because he gradually loses himself and as a result he loses her as well."

"In turn, women then also become alienated from themselves and feel guilty about being who they really are. Many of you, both women and men, have been stuck in this illusion for the past two thousand years. This situation is repeated, confirmed and illustrated in all possible ways, for instance in movies, television series, plays and music. There is another trend as well; a new consciousness that strives to heal the female and male principles on Earth, and this has made it possible for us to discuss this theme today."

Sexuality is also sacred

"Through my image as the mother Mary, an idealised picture of motherhood was presented in the Bible, in the New Testament, that is basically not of this Earth. I am supposed to have been impregnated by the Holy Spirit, but never been joined sexually with a man. This assumption has caused a certain amount of loneliness. The female principle is considered sinful; basically, it is allowed to exist only partially, namely as the maternal aspect. This division indeed had a purpose, in terms of human development and evolution, but it is now time for unity and integration. Women who take me as an example still become confused. If they want to be a mother, they have to become 'unclean' by joining with a man and this also makes the man sinful. Often, deep down, they then feel guilty about conceiving a child by means of sexual contact. However, at the same time, this energy of guilt is passed on to the unborn child. The assumption is then: 'We women are no good and so neither are you'."

"This locks out any growth of the human consciousness. Where is the key? It lies in respect for and appreciation of the female principle. The creative principle that manifests itself between man and woman is basically of a Divine nature. It is a magic moment, a moment in which 'Heaven and Earth' meet as a passageway enabling the spirit to manifest itself on Earth as a human being. The consciousness of the parents plays a key role in this. What makes a relationship pure or impure, what makes sexuality pure or impure? Through the connection with the heart, the love that the man and woman feel for themselves and for each other, one becomes increasingly more aware of the presence of the Divine. And at the right moment, sexual intercourse can then be an opportunity for conceiving a child, but also for experiencing unity."

"For a long time, sexuality was called a sin and labelled unclean. But is it really? If we interpret the word *sin* as confusion, loneliness, pain, being unfulfilled, we can discover another dimension for this term because the unification between man and woman that manifests itself on a physical, emotional, mental and spiritual level can be a pre-eminent source of bliss. Yet people can also experience intense pain and suffering while growing towards each other. But if people enter into a relationship with love for each other and also love for themselves, in which the latter is the basis for the love for each other, then this relationship can be a source of fulfilment, love, happiness and inspiration for themselves and for the other. One feels fulfilled in one's heart and from this fulfilment one grows in the relationship to experience a more profound level of unity."

"If you are not in harmony with yourself and you enter into the relationship with an attitude of dependency in order to find fulfilment in the other, you intensify that inner pain; in this respect you could speak of 'sin'! I say this without a hint of accusation, but with understanding and compassion. It could be that you need this pain in order to be able to return to yourself, as is often the case."

Joseph as an example to men

"The essence of being a woman is receptiveness; this is what the female principle represents in the world. All that exists must first be received before it can take shape. Receiving gives the woman peace, self-confidence and appreciation. The male principle gives, builds and protects what it has built. Joseph is a builder. He created all the necessary circumstances for me to receive Jesus in me."

"The love between Joseph and me is unconditional, also in the spiritual dimension we are in now. We are an example to human couples. Completely equal. Men can learn much from Joseph; they can follow his example. He can advise as to how a man should treat a woman, namely with much respect, love and admiration. If a man is able to appreciate his wife completely in his heart and vice versa, those two can enjoy a blissful flow of love between them and spread that love all over the world. This love is without ego. Jesus was begot and born under these pure circumstances; this is an example to show that such a man/woman relationship enables Him to be born in your heart. I will say more about this below."

Merging in Divine love

"When it is said that Jesus was begot without 'sin', through Immaculate Conception as it is called, it really means that my relationship with Joseph was determined by unconditional love and that personal interests played no part in this. We were prepared for the coming of Jesus long before. We were purified at all levels. All our energy centres and energy bodies were totally attuned to each other (see Revelation 23) and at the highest level of Divine consciousness. We can say that at that moment Joseph and I no longer existed as individuals. We were entirely merged in Divine love that by definition is impersonal. In this pure state, God gave us and the world Jesus via the Holy Spirit. I want to make it clear that both Joseph and I were necessary to make this Divine process possible. Being able to merge in Divine love is the highest and purest level that a man/woman relationship can achieve on Earth. Certainly, this pure state for intercourse is not necessary by definition to be able to beget and give birth to a child, but it is the most ideal circumstance. It is also one of the most ideal conditions to awaken the Christ-consciousness in our heart. The intense longing that millions of people on Earth have for such a loving relationship makes this pure intercourse right for them."

Jesus was also begot physically

"You may wonder whether Jesus was conceived physically. The answer is yes! You see, the physical level is also a Divine level and this only makes the unification in Divine love and with the Holy Spirit more complete. The message ensuing from this event is that Heaven and Earth can be completely one and completely integrated and this is how it should be. One level corresponds with the other and it also mirrors the male and female principles. Stressing the absence of physical conception would not do Mother Earth justice. Mother Earth adds female 'receptive' energy and the Holy Spirit adds the male 'impregnating' energy to this relationship. Joseph and I are instruments of this Divine unification."

"However, a condition is attached to this process. Both partners must be aware of their own Divine nature. You opted to consider me as a symbol of purity. You used to consider sexuality as something impure; many people still look at it as such. This assumption is stored in the collective subconsciousness. The only way to give me a pure identity was to call me a virgin. If I were to be impregnated by Joseph I would lose my holiness and that would then be true, as it were, for every woman. And in this view, the man would also be someone who can deprive the woman of her holiness. Naturally, there is no room for love, for unification, for real connection in such a situation. There is also no room for loving conception. It is as if a curse were to rest on a moment which in itself is holy. And this estrangement penetrates the consciousness of the foetus. And so every person on Earth is born with a sense of guilt. This subtle manipulation of the truth is a special form of slavery that has caused the power of man to be 'locked up'. In the time of Jesus, mankind was in a process in which consciousness and power were decreasing. At that time, they could not deal very well with their own aggression, for instance, nor could they give sexuality the place it actually should have, namely as a connection between sexuality and the heart centre so that sexuality is driven primarily by the power of love instead of by the power of the ego or by playing out unsolved emotional patterns. If sexuality is driven by the power of love from the heart, then that is the basis of a process that subsequently leads to more profound connections between sexuality and higher states of consciousness. This connection between sexuality and love is a prerequisite for healing mankind and creating a happy life on Earth. Mankind's relationship with aggression, with sexuality and with the process of dying is the main thing that should be healed at this time. These three elements must connect with the heart."

"It is important to add that you were not a victim in the process of consciousness reduction. This process played a very important role in your collective development and also in your awakening."

The conception and the Revelation of Gabriel

Mary: "You may wonder how you should interpret the story in the Bible about Jesus' conception and my relationship with Joseph. To do so we must place ourselves in that time. Joseph and I had a very strong mental bond. When we were actually drawn to each other physically by the will of God, a profound bond of love was activated between us. A short period of time passed before we realised that we were meant for each other. And that we had a unique feeling of oneness."

"Various events took place in this glorious feeling. The time has now come to turn our attention to these events. For instance, how was my encounter with Archangel Gabriel? Gabriel first came to me and told me that Joseph would beget a child by me with the ratification of the Holy Spirit. Three important prerequisites were at hand for this, namely:

1. the basis for the birth in the form of the individuals Joseph and Mary and the higher powers that were incarnated in them;
2. the highly developed spirit of Jesus himself;
3. the initiation of Jesus, Joseph and Mary by the Holy Spirit."

"Gabriel also showed me the important events that would take place in the life of Jesus and how we would have to support him in difficult times. He also showed me the deeper significance of the important moments in Jesus' life. Gabriel gave Joseph a dream in which he, too, could take in this information. He sensed God's approval to take me, Mary, to be his wife. Gabriel brought us together once and for all, after which we could experience the Divine unity. Jesus was conceived in this pure love with the intense blessing and guidance of the Holy Spirit."

Mary: "The Biblical version as you know it, namely that Jesus was born of a virgin, is how the people of those days interpreted these events. This was because mankind was not ready to accept the purity of woman and a pure and equal relationship between man and woman. In those days people assumed that the purity of the woman was linked to her virginity."

"Gabriel also told me that at a given time the world would be ready for the truth. Then mankind would be able to receive and accept the truth. That time has now come."

"Mary Magdalene and the apostles were aware of all this. The male apostles, with the exception of John, later accepted the official version as the truth because they had a greater affinity with that interpretation and also because they found it difficult to accept the equality of man and woman."

The holy heart

"Let us now look at the purity of the female principle. I am not pure because I am a virgin, but because I am completely aware of my holiness as a woman. And my heart is the predominant energy in my existence. Through my heart I am one with the universe and I am – always and everywhere – never alone. I represent the power of the Heavenly Mother who connects Heaven and Earth so that they can fertilise each other. That is what is holy. This does not take place from the ego, but from the heart. Those who are touched by this statement can best pray to me and I will help to make this subject and the process that they experience with respect to this subject clear in their human hearts. You do not need an intermediary for this, I am here for you, all you have to do is call me and I will guide you along. I do not recommend that you enter into intellectual discussions on this subject because you will get confused and lose sight of the essence. This subject must not be approached from the ego, but from the heart. Sharing your experiences with others from your heart can enrich you. Every door has a key and the key to this subject lies hidden within the heart; you can always summon me from there."

Resolving the guilt

"Many people carry within them the subtle message 'I am not allowed to be here on Earth'. This is because the following process has taken place: the sexuality of the mother is not permitted (she is not pure), the sexuality of the father is not permitted (he deprives the woman of her purity). And so the sexuality of the parents is actually not permitted. This means that the contact between the parents is not permitted. The child is the fruit of this contact. If the contact between the parents is not permitted, this in fact means that the child is not permitted either. Mankind is dominated subtly by this belief."

"This obstructs the connection, the unification between man and woman. Resolving the guilt concerning your conception is the key to solving your aggression, frustration and fear of death. And this is an important step on the way to being aware of your heart on Earth in order to be able to realise and manifest the Divinity within you through a relationship. Jesus and his 'team' activated mankind's energy of the heart. Even if human beings belonging to a former civilisation also had an open heart, the arrival of the Christ-energy on Earth added a new dimension to it, namely, the dimension of compassion and forgiveness."

"The essence of the transformation is that both women and men can feel their own Divinity and love themselves unconditionally. This acceptance within opens the heart to one's love for each other, which is the basis for an unconditional conception. A conception that enables and allows the child to be entirely itself."

"The arrival of the Christ-energy on Earth introduced a permanent change; it can be said that the heart has been successfully transformed. It is like a seed that is planted in the heart and develops when the time is ripe for each individual."

Relationship as a way to the Christ-consciousness

"Sexual energy is a powerful instrument; if this energy is centred entirely on the heart one obtains access to higher love dimensions of the Divine by connecting with each other at all levels. If the sexual energy is not connected with the heart it can only cause confusion, loneliness, agitation and a feeling of searching in the dark and one loses oneself. Some people are in a certain stage of development in which they themselves can connect their own sexual energy with higher energy centres without a physical partner. These people make partners of mankind in general and nature in particular. This can sometimes also be connected with the fact that their closest soul mate has not yet incarnated on Earth.
The connection between man and woman on an energetic level can bring about a perfect merge that can result in an awakening of the Christ-energy. In fact, this can be achieved through any kind of relationship involving the heart. Loving relationships result in the possibility of connections without ego as a way to unconditional love and to a higher state of consciousness; an awakening of the Christ-consciousness in every heart. Every kind of interpersonal relationship, such as a friendship, a parent-child relationship, homosexual

partnerships, as well as friendly relationships with animals and nature in general can lead to an awakening of the Christ-consciousness in the heart."

"Some people feel attracted to a partner of the same sex. This can open their heart wide for them and help to release the Christ-consciousness in their hearts. These people opted for this at the level of their soul. The reasons for this can be multifarious in nature and linked to the evolutionary path of the soul in its development over various planetary and solar systems."

"The acceptance of homosexuality on Earth is currently still in progress. The fact that homosexual couples can get married opens up new dimensions of the heart at a collective level. Society is warming to accepting various kinds of interpersonal attachments. This gives proof of a development that has been initiated lately by homosexual relationships for the people who are involved themselves and for society. It is a kind of pioneering work."

"Those who are born homosexual must really assert their own sexuality and also stand by their own love. If one has not been able to do this for whatever reason in a former life, this provides the opportunity to remedy it. Marrying each other is the ritual that blesses the choice for each other at a social and a Divine level. This is because the partners involved have broken through all fears and judgements concerning their love, they can fully accept themselves and their partner and they can share their love for each other with others."

Accepting others opens up the heart

"People have wasted, through ignorance, a lot of energy in resisting and rejecting these kinds of attachments, which has only created more tension and loneliness on Earth. People who choose a 'different' path give others the opportunity to open their hearts wider and to shift the limits of love and compassion. You see, you people tend to love people and accept them sooner when they resemble you. And you feel more involved with people who have the same sexual nature and political preference or who are of the same race or who belong to the same football club. You find it easier to connect with them because you recognise yourself in them. When other people hold up a mirror for you in which you cannot easily recognise yourself (different colour, religion, other sexual preference, etc.) you feel a certain fear on a conscious or subconscious level. In order to accept these people you must overcome your inhibitions and open yourself up more. When you acknowledge them as they really are, a connection is created at an essential level of the heart. This connection from heart to heart is not dependent on the above-mentioned characteristics such as race, colour and religion. Try it! The exercise below is aimed at helping you to open your heart in this respect.

Exercise for accepting the Divinity in yourself and in others

• Withdraw to a quiet place.

• Keep your attention focused on yourself.

• Breathe deeply into the belly and feel how you relax.

• Abandon all ideas and thoughts.

• If your attention turns to your thoughts, bring it gently back to your heart.

• Feel how that feels.

• Explore yourself. Become aware of yourself.

• Accept yourself completely as you are.

• Repeat to yourself 'I am God'.

• Feel how it feels to say that.

• Acknowledge your own Divinity.

• Admire yourself.

• Then select a person who seems 'entirely different' from you.

• Accept this person completely by acknowledging that he or she is also God.

• Open yourself to experience the Divinity in this person.

• Repeat to yourself '...........is God'.

• Acknowledge the Divinity in that person.

• Admire that person.

• Turn your attention to your heart and close an imaginary love contract between your heart and this person until you experience a clear connection.

• Continue until you feel love flow from your heart to the person you selected.

• Continue until you feel a loving unity between the person you selected and yourself.

• Breathe deeply into the belly and connect with your body again.

• Slowly open your eyes and return to the here and now.

• Do this exercise as often as possible in all sorts of circumstances and with all sorts of people, even those that you love the least."

Mary as a sister

"Besides the principle of mother and wife, I also represent the sister principle. This principle is not linked to the interaction between woman and man. It is universal in nature and reflects the unity of all people on Earth. As a sister of all people I am unconditional towards you and I love you like my own family. We are an entity, we are God. In our Divinity we are equal and we help each other to realise a common goal, namely to let the Christ-consciousness awaken on Earth. Compassion is central in the sister principle. Developing compassion for yourself and for everything and everyone will awaken the Christ in your heart. We share this source of bliss with each other."

Revelation 12

Mary Magdalene about the sacred meaning of menstruation, about men 'giving' and women 'receiving' as a crucial element in their relationship, about her loving partnership with Jesus that they want to reveal to the world and the significance that the two of them can have as a couple for every man and woman. Exercise to call up Mary Magdalene and Jesus in your heart.

Mary Magdalene: "I would now like to focus on a special time in the life of a woman, namely her monthly cycle. When she menstruates, she is in a special state of consciousness in which she is in stronger contact with her 'higher self' than usual. In this state she inadvertently obtains access to the Divine world and to higher dimensions. And a merge occurs with the principle that I represent. You see, I am in every woman and every woman is in me. The holiness of the woman emerges most strongly during her menstrual period. And she should be honoured for this. If a man honours his wife at this special time he also comes into stronger contact with his higher self. This concerted action is a door to the Cosmos, as it were. It is a time at which a woman can withdraw and unwind in order to experience the connection with her higher self and with the Divine dimension of being a woman. When the woman creates space for herself in this way, she also creates room for her partner. So that they form an entity and can journey together to their Divine consciousness. The woman creates the opening through which the couple can pass."

"If they do not unwind they do not become aware, or become only partially aware, of this spiritual opening. They feel less comfortable, are irritated and get off balance. They experience their menstruation as an obstacle instead of an opportunity. And this negative aspect becomes an element of tension in their relationship whereas it can be an element of unification."

Man gives, woman receives

"It is important for a woman that she remains in contact with her intrinsic essence and that she fosters this essence. Because when a woman is in balance she can radiate her own Divinity, which makes her a source of inspiration for her partner and for others. She opens channels of consciousness in her partner, making them able to experience, acknowledge and manifest the deeper mysteries of life in society. I would like to mention a few here:

• The mystery of the creation of life

• Experiencing the Divine consciousness

• Being the instrument of a larger whole

• The mystery of the cycles of nature

• The mystery of resolving the ego

• The mystery of giving and receiving

• The mystery of resolving the cycle of death and birth

• Total submission

• Experiencing unity

• Experiencing unconditional love

• Experiencing the unity between substance and consciousness

• Conquering the illusion of the material, emotional and mental world"

"Women sometimes lose contact with their inner self and then assume a pose to find their inner self in the man. They then expect to find a certain fulfilment in him that is in fact in themselves. If this happens, both partners feel lonely and unsatisfied. This often puzzles the woman. She says. 'I have given him everything and now he is leaving.' It is now time to heal this aspect in order to discover the true values of giving and receiving. You see, the essence of the woman is receiving; the essence of the man is giving. This balance manifests itself in everything that exists. The man 'fertilises' the woman in the broad sense of the term and receives from her in return all sorts of 'fruits', which nourishes and inspires him and motivates him to give to her and fertilise her again. And the latter happens at all levels of consciousness. Again, 'fertilising' in this case is meant in the broad sense of the term; in certain instances it can literally mean begetting a child but it also has to do with a physical, energetic, emotional and mental process in the communication back and forth between man and woman. A woman who gives to a man without first having received from him quickly becomes tired, empty and sad; she loses herself. Perhaps you know this feeling. In essence, women feel happy when they receive, men feel happy when they give. A woman who has received can give her husband much love in response which in turn makes him feel nourished. Just look at relationships that are harmonious and happy."

Mary Magdalene was not a whore

"In the course of time, many people have made me out to be a whore, but I am not a whore. And I have never been one, although I am present in all women, including those who work as prostitutes. I do not wish to discriminate in this. For me, all women are equal. I embrace them all in my heart."

"During my incarnation in the time of Jesus I was an independent woman. I felt my own connection with God and was faithful to God. In the same way I am always faithful to Jesus. Our relationship is timeless. We have always been together and we always shall be. It has no beginning and no end because we are one in Divine consciousness. Our incarnation at that time had a specific plan and an important purpose for mankind, namely activating the Christ-consciousness in the human heart."

"Women were either very attracted to me or were afraid of me in that period. This depended on how they dealt with being a woman. Many men in that time wanted to dominate me but they could not. They felt insecure in my presence. I felt a lot of compassion for them."

"That time was strongly dominated by men and the female principle was not properly integrated in society. People found it difficult to place me. Some men reacted with anger and incomprehension. As an expression of these feelings they called me a 'whore'. This was an attempt to deny and arrest the female principle in themselves. But I cannot be halted because I live in every heart and also in their heart. The time was not yet ripe to open their hearts to me. The time has now arrived for that. Both then and now, all this was and is a part of the Divine play in which we perform a perfect role together with you."

Mary Magdalene and Jesus as a couple

"'Whoever has ears to hear, let him hear; whoever has eyes to see, let him see.' This Biblical saying fits perfectly with the relationship between Jesus and me. I have the honour of being allowed to receive from the Lord and I have been allowed to nourish and inspire the son of God and to love him. For him, our relationship is a safe basis in which he can fuel himself in order to manifest his message for the world. And the whole world has absorbed the love between the two of us; just as the sun shines so do we. Our unity cannot be divided. Jesus has always protected me against the lack of understanding of others. The world is now ripe to acknowledge us as a couple. This may create a sensation among people and start a lot of commotion. This is part of the process. It has to do with the deep purification that is now needed and places the female principle back in the spotlight after thousands of years of denial. The love and respect that man and woman are supposed to give each other are a clear direction for all those who feel so inclined. Let this register: become aware of your resistances, should you have any, but leave the process to its own devices. Accept us together in your heart and let the female and male principles in yourself, both man and woman, come into balance."

"We are present in every person. If one principle is more obvious, such as the Jesus aspect in a man and me in a woman, then the other principle is more in the background. I am also present in men as their access to feelings and inspiration in order for them to open up to the Divine. Jesus is also present in every woman, namely as a source of power and protection for themselves. Together we represent unconditional love. In life we were allowed to receive the Christ-energy and every man and woman is capable of this as soon as they are pure in their heart. To purify the heart one must be able to transcend various aspects of the ego. This process needs time and cannot be forced. If you are willing, we will guide you on this road to initiation. To do so, you must accept us in your heart, you must open yourselves to our light and our love, which is also your own light and love, and to all that we can do for you."

Exercise – Mary Magdalene and Jesus in your heart

"The following exercise will help you awaken us in your heart.

• Withdraw to a quiet place.

- Close your eyes.

- Breathe deeply into the belly and feel how you relax.

- Turn your attention to your heart.

- Repeat the Prayer to Christ in your heart.

Lord Jesus Christ
Son of God
Have mercy upon me
Amen

- Let it register.

- Now repeat the prayer to Mary Magdalene to yourself.

Dear Mary Magdalene
Divine woman
Have mercy upon me
And awaken in me
Help me to heal and appreciate the female principle within me
In all the depths of my being, in my fellow man and in everything
on Earth
Amen

- Visualise Jesus and Mary Magdalene standing beside each other in front of you as a Divine couple.

- Let them slowly enter your heart and embrace them.

- Feel the flow of love between you and them.

- Feel the unity with them in your heart.

- Feel in your heart the integration between the female and the male principles in perfect harmony.

- Let this harmony flow through your whole body.

- Enjoy it.

- Breathe deeply into the belly and connect again with your body.

- Slowly open your eyes and return to the here and now."

Revelation 13

Mary Magdalene gives exercises and prayers for the healing of the woman, for the healing of the emotional and mental body, for the healing of the relationship of the man with his physical body and for the restoration of the relationship with people with whom you have a negative connection.

Mary Magdalene: "Dear brothers and sisters, I am very happy that we are together again. I am the unknown. Only now is there room for me in your heart. I know that we have longed deeply for each other for a long time. Now is the time for integration, for recognition; a time that I may share in my heart with you all and that you may share with me. We, the spiritual masters of the White Brother- and Sisterhood, are representatives of certain aspects of the Divine power and the Divine love that are also present in every person. When we 'speak' with you, you must not see us just as 'individuals', but also as forces of consciousness and love. My force, the energy that I represent, is also a part of your heart. I represent the female principle. This principle is present in the woman's relationship with herself, in the partnership with a man, in the man's relationship with himself, in the devotion to the spiritual process and also in the relationship with all brothers and sisters on Earth. Healings take place on all these levels. And this is the purpose of the following exercises."

Exercise 1 – Healing of the woman's relationship with her body

"I would like to start with the healing of the female aspect in every woman. So this is an exercise for women.

• Wear feminine clothing, preferably a dress or a skirt.

• Withdraw to a quiet place where you cannot be disturbed and make yourself comfortable.

• Repeat the Prayer to Mary Magdalene three times.

• Close your eyes.

• Breathe deeply into the belly and feel how you relax.

• Intently explore your entire body.

• Feel and become aware of the acceptance of or resistance to different parts of your body.

• Examine whether emotions are linked to this acceptance or resistance.

• If there is resistance, become aware of the underlying fear that is the source of this resistance.

• Feel this fear. And befriend this fear with love.

• Accept the fear with compassion and objectively. This fear has a purpose. Fear also has a positive purpose.

• Open yourself up to recognise and experience the positive purpose this fear has for you. What can you learn from it?

• Look for and define a way other than the fear to fulfil this purpose.

• Let go of the fear. Should this be difficult for you, transfer the fear to me.

- Pay special attention to your female organs, such as your vagina, uterus, ovaries and breasts.

- Repeat this exercise until you feel total acceptance of your body.

- If you have a lot of difficulty with some parts of your body or if some parts of your body are linked to one or more painful experiences, use the Prayer to Mary Magdalene and focus it on that specific body part with a special variation, for instance:

Dear Mary Magdalene
Divine woman
Have mercy upon my womb and awaken in my womb
And help my womb to heal and appreciate the female principle
within me
In all the depths of my being
In my fellow man
And in everything on Earth
Amen

Variations to the Prayer to Mary Magdalene can also be applied to organs that have been removed. The relevant organ, that is no longer present in its physical form, can thus still be healed in your consciousness.

Exercise 2 – The man's acceptance of his body

The purpose of this exercise is to heal, by means of the female principle, the man's relationship with his physical body and thus connect the male body to his heart.

- Find a quiet place where you cannot be disturbed and make yourself comfortable.

• Repeat the Prayer to Mary Magdalene three times.

Dear Mary Magdalene
Divine woman
Have mercy upon me and awaken in me
Help me to heal and appreciate the female principle within me
In all the depths of my being, in my fellow man and in everything
on Earth
Amen

• Close your eyes.

• Breathe deeply into the belly and feel how you relax.

• Intently explore your entire body.

• Feel and become aware of the acceptance of or resistance to different parts of your body.

• Examine whether emotions are linked to this acceptance or resistance.

• If there is resistance, become aware of the underlying fear that is the source of this resistance.

• Feel this fear. And befriend this fear with love.

• Accept the fear with compassion and objectively. This fear has a purpose. Fear also has a positive purpose.

• Open yourself up to recognise and experience the positive purpose this fear has for you. What can you learn from it?

• Look for and define a way other than the fear to fulfil this purpose.

• Let go of the fear. Should this be difficult for you, transfer the fear to me.

• Pay special attention to your male organs.

• Repeat this exercise until you feel total acceptance of your body.

Exercise 3 – Healing of the emotional awareness

I would like to continue with the healing of the emotional awareness of both men and women.

• Close your eyes.

• Breathe deeply into the belly and feel how you relax.

• Intently explore your entire body and your emotions.

• Open yourself up to all sorts of memories, experiences and convictions that generate strong emotions. Which emotions are most emphatically present?

• Be aware of the connection of each emotion with certain parts of your body. Examine which emotions are connected to which body parts.

• Make a loving connection with each of these emotions from your heart. Picture it as a stream of golden liquid love flowing from your heart to that emotion and those body parts. Accept each emotion with an open heart.

• Apply the Prayer to Mary Magdalene to emotions that generate too much tension. Do this until you are resigned to them and you have fully accepted them with love.

Exercise 4 – Healing of the mental body

The mental body of both man and woman needs healing as well.

• Take an opinion that you have of yourself.

• Repeat this several times in your mind.

• Feel what it is like to have such an opinion.

• Does the opinion evoke certain emotions?

• Feel the emotions that the opinion evokes in you.

• Breathe deeply into the belly and let the emotions be. Give them free reign.

• Repeat the opinion several times in your mind.

• Can you feel the opinion in one or more parts of your body?

• Does the opinion evoke certain physical sensations?

• Breathe deeply into the belly and let these physical sensations be. Give them free reign.

• Repeat the opinion several more times in your mind.

• Feel the connection between your opinion, your emotions and your physical sensations and the parts of your body.

• Breathe deeply into the belly and feel how that feels.

• Accept this experience fully.

• Feel whether you want to keep the opinion or whether you want to let it go.

• If you want to keep the opinion, be aware of the emotions and the physical sensations that the opinion evokes and opt for this completely.

• If you want to let go of the opinion, transfer it to me by means of the Prayer to Mary Magdalene.

Dear Mary Magdalene
Divine woman
Have mercy upon me and take away from me the opinion that
.....
And awaken in me
Help me to heal and appreciate the female principle within me
In all the depths of my being, in my fellow man and in everything
on Earth
Amen

If a certain opinion, emotion or body part generates too much tension, you can apply the Prayer to Mary Magdalene to it. If other prayers enter your mind for a certain part of this exercise, such as the Prayer to Christ or the Prayer to Mary, do not hesitate to apply these prayers; they are then, at that moment, the most suitable for that specific experience.

Exercise 5 – Applying the Prayer to Mary Magdalene to others

If there are men or women in your surroundings with whom you have a positive or a negative relationship, you can apply the Prayer to Mary Magdalene to these people as follows. I have taken your mother as a random example of a negative connection.

Dear Mary Magdalene
Divine woman
Have mercy upon my mother and awaken in her
Help my mother to heal and appreciate the female principle
within her
In all the depths of her being, in her fellow man and in everything
on Earth
Amen

When you are finished with these various healings you can recite the original Prayer to Mary Magdalene three times in closing."

Dear Mary Magdalene
Divine woman
Have mercy upon me and awaken in me
Help me to heal and appreciate the female principle within me
In all the depths of my being, in my fellow man and in everything
on Earth
Amen

Revelation 14

Mary's exercises for solving fears.

Mary: "You may wonder how the principles we gave you in the previous Revelations work in daily practice. To explain this I will now discuss one of the most essential emotional and psychological dimensions of man, namely fear. I would like to give you some exercises for coping with fear. Fear is one of the emotions most present in mankind on Earth. Before starting on the exercises, I would like you to say the Prayer to Mary three times."

Dear Mary
Divine mother of Heaven and Earth
Have mercy upon me
Awaken the love in my heart for all that exists and for myself
Help me to live with an open mind like a Divine child
That is amazed about everything
And that treats everything in this Heavenly paradise with love
and respect
Help me to let my Divine essence awaken completely
To be who I actually am in Heaven and on Earth
And that your love and my love, dear Mother, may be one
For now and forever
Amen

Exercise 1 – Becoming conscious of fear and love

"In order to make things clear, I would like you to focus your attention on the following two principles:

(1) Fear is the source of violence and (2) fear is the source of resistance.

1.1 Fear is the source of violence

• Withdraw to a quiet place.

• Close your eyes.

• Breathe deeply into the belly and feel how you relax.

• Repeat to yourself: 'Fear is the source of violence'.

• Breathe deeply into the belly and be still.

• Which parts of your body react to your saying this principle?

• Experience this and let it register.

• Look for examples of fear that have led to violence in your own life.

• Breathe deeply into the belly and be still.

• Experience this and let it register.

• Turn your attention to your heart and feel the unconditional love that is in your heart.

• Let this love flow from your heart to every cell.

• Let your fear dissolve in this love.

• Visualise a connection between your tailbone and the centre of the Earth.

- Let yourself be borne by Mother Earth.

- Feel how the Earth bears you.

- Visualise a link between the crown of your head and a universal source of unconditional love, the Christ-energy.

- Let yourself be borne by this universal love.

- Feel how this universal love bears you.

- Take your time to experience this.

- Feel your breathing again.

- When you are ready, open your eyes.

1.2 Fear is the source of resistance

- Withdraw to a quiet place.

- Close your eyes.

- Breathe deeply into the belly and feel how you relax.

- Repeat to yourself: 'Fear is the source of resistance'.

- Breathe deeply into the belly and be still.

- Which parts of your body react to your saying this principle?

- Experience this and let it register.

- Look for examples of fear that led to resistance in your own life.

• Breathe deeply into the belly and be still.

• Experience this and let it register.

• Turn your attention to your heart and feel the unconditional love that is in your heart.

• Let this love flow from your heart to every cell.

• Let your fear dissolve in this love.

• Visualise a link between your tailbone and the centre of the Earth.

• Let yourself be borne by Mother Earth.

• Feel how the Earth bears you.

• Visualise a link between the crown of your head and a universal source of unconditional love, the Christ-energy.

• Let yourself be borne by this universal love.

• Feel how this universal love bears you.

• Take your time to experience this.

• Feel your breathing again.

• When you are ready, open your eyes.

Exercise 2 – Becoming conscious of the effect of fear

The purpose of the following exercises is to let you become conscious of the effect of fear when you let aggressive feelings and resistances develop within yourself, towards yourself as well as towards others.

2.1 Aggressive feelings within yourself towards someone else

• Withdraw to a quiet place and close your eyes.

• Breathe deeply into the belly and feel how you relax.

• Look for aggressive feelings within yourself towards someone else.

• Become aware of the fear that is the source of your aggression.

• Feel this fear. And have mercy upon this fear with love.

• Accept this fear with compassion, objectively. It has a function.

• Open yourself to experience the positive function of this fear.

• Look for and define a way other than this fear to fulfil this function.

• Turn your attention to your heart and feel the unconditional love that is in your heart.

• Let this love flow from your heart to every cell.

• Let your fear dissolve in this love. Should this be difficult, transfer your fear to me by means of the following Prayer to Mary.

Dear Mary,
Divine mother of Heaven and Earth
Have mercy upon me
And take over from me all my fears and aggressive feelings
Let compassion and unconditional love flow in my heart
To myself
To my fellow man
And to everything on Earth
Amen

- Feel your breathing again.

- When you are ready, open your eyes.

You can replace the words 'to my fellow man' in the Prayer to Mary by the name of a specific person with whom you have difficulties.

2.2 Aggressive feelings about yourself or about certain aspects of yourself

- Withdraw to a quiet place.

- Close your eyes.

- Breathe deeply into the belly and feel how you relax.

- Look for aggressive feelings about yourself or about certain aspects of yourself.

- Become aware of the fear that is the source of these aggressive feelings.

- Feel this fear. And have mercy upon this fear with love.

- Accept this fear with compassion, objectively. It has a function.

- Open yourself to experience the positive function of this fear.

- Look for and define a way other than this fear to fulfil this function.

- Turn your attention to your heart and feel the unconditional love that is in your heart.

- Let this love flow from your heart to every cell.

• Let your fear dissolve in this love. Should this be difficult, transfer your fear to me by means of the Prayer to Mary.

Dear Mary,
Divine mother of Heaven and Earth
Have mercy upon me
And take over from me all my fears and aggressive feelings
Let compassion and unconditional love flow in my heart
To myself
To my fellow man
And to everything on Earth
Amen

• Feel your breathing again.

• When you are ready, open your eyes.

You can replace the words 'to my fellow man' in the Prayer to Mary by specific aspects of yourself with which you have problems.

2.3 Resistance towards a certain experience

• Withdraw to a quiet place.

• Close your eyes.

• Breathe deeply into the belly and feel how you relax.

• Look for resistance towards a certain experience.

• Become aware of the fear that is the source of this resistance.

• Feel this fear. And have mercy upon this fear with love.

• Accept this fear with compassion, objectively. It has a function.

• Open yourself to experience the positive function of this fear.

• Look for and define a way other than this fear to fulfil this function.

• Turn your attention to your heart and feel the unconditional love that is in your heart.

• Let this love flow from your heart to every cell.

• Let your fear dissolve in this love. Should this be difficult, transfer your fear to me by means of the Prayer to Mary as mentioned previously.

• Feel your breathing again.

• When you are ready, open your eyes.

If you find it difficult to recognise your aggression or resistance, do the following exercise.

2.4 Someone about whom you have a negative opinion

• Withdraw to a quiet place.

• Close your eyes.

• Breathe deeply into the belly and feel how you relax.

• Look for someone about whom you have a negative opinion.

• Become aware of the fear that is the source of this opinion.

• Feel this fear. And have mercy upon this fear with love.

- Accept this fear with compassion, objectively. It has a function.

- Open yourself to experience the positive function of this fear.

- Look for and define a way other than this fear to fulfil this function.

- Turn your attention to your heart and feel the unconditional love that is in your heart.

- Let this love flow from your heart to every cell.

- Let your fear dissolve in this love. Should this be difficult, transfer your fear to me by means of the Prayer to Mary as mentioned previously.

- Feel your breathing again.

- When you are ready, open your eyes.

2.5 A situation in which you feel you are a victim

- Withdraw to a quiet place.

- Close your eyes.

- Breathe deeply into the belly and feel how you relax.

- Look for a situation in which you feel you are a victim.

- Become aware of the fear that is the source of this feeling of being a victim.

- Feel this fear. And have mercy upon this fear with love.

- Accept this fear with compassion, objectively. It has a function.

• Open yourself to experience the positive function of this fear.

• Look for and define a way other than this fear to fulfil this function.

• Turn your attention to your heart and feel the unconditional love that is in your heart.

• Let this love flow from your heart to every cell.

• Let your fear dissolve in this love. Should this be difficult, transfer your fear to me by means of the Prayer to Mary as mentioned previously.

• Feel your breathing again.

• When you are ready, open your eyes.

Exercise 3 - Healing the feeling of being a victim/offender

The purpose of this exercise is to heal the feeling of being a victim/offender that is present around all forms of aggression and resistance. A connection is laid from heart to heart that fulfils the underlying need for love and recognition.

• Withdraw to a quiet place.

• Close your eyes.

• Breathe deeply into the belly and feel how you relax.

• Look for a situation in the past or in the present in which you have experienced or experience discrimination, aggression, violence or resistance towards you by others.

• Relive how it feels to be treated that way.

- Feel these feelings. And have mercy upon these feelings with love.

- Accept these feelings with compassion, objectively. They have a function.

- Open yourself to experience the positive function of these feelings.

- Look for and define a way other than these feelings to fulfil this function.

- Let these feelings go. Should this be difficult, transfer them to me by means of the following prayer:

Dear Mary,
Divine mother of Heaven and Earth
Have mercy upon me
And take over from me all my fears and aggressive feelings
Let compassion and unconditional love flow in my heart
To myself
To .... (the name of the person you see as the offender)
And to everything on Earth
Amen

- Turn your attention to the person who discriminates or attacks you or towards whom you feel resistance.

- Become aware of the fear caused by the aggressive behaviour of this person.

- Make contact with the fear in the other person. Feel how afraid this person is of you. Afraid of you and of what you show him or her or let him or her feel. Afraid of the possibilities that you entail.

- Feel how it feels to feel this fear in the other person.

• Turn your attention back to your heart and make a connection between your own heart and the fear of this fellow man and have mercy upon this scared person with love and accept the fear in that person.

• Make a loving connection between your own heart and the heart of the other person.

• Let the love between the two hearts flow until you begin to smile.

• Feel your breathing again.

• When you are ready, open your eyes."

Revelation 15

Jesus and Mary Magdalene about the road to the initiation of man on Earth. The first three of ten steps with accompanying exercises for breaking out of the illusion of being isolated, for putting the ego into perspective and for restoring the love for oneself.

Jesus and Mary Magdalene: "When a soul is on the way to a three-dimensional existence here on Earth, certain transformations take place in its consciousness. These transformations are a consequence of becoming part of matter. At the moment that the soul assumes a material frame, a human body – that is to say, when it incarnates – the soul also takes with it the essence of an energetic, emotional and mental body. All these bodies are built up and developed further during life 'in the flesh', in matter. Together, they form the essence of the human ego. The ego is a frame of consciousness that gives man the illusion of being isolated from the universe, from God, from everything that exists. This illusion is the main cause of pain, illness, misfortune and misery in the world. Yet the ego has a function. The ego is necessary for man to develop on Earth, for being able to experience life in time and space, the three-dimensional state. We can welcome the ego into our heart, because the ego also needs loving acknowledgement. By accepting and acknowledging the ego, the ego becomes prepared to surrender to the love of the heart."

"There comes a time in a person's life when he or she discovers there is something wrong with the illusion of being isolated; it does not correspond with the desire for unity, the desire for contact, the desire for love. Sometimes this need is given shape in someone's quest through physical sexuality. A quest that, without further spiritual contact, ends in a dead end and unfulfilment. It is that person's task to reconnect with the whole through love. Love is the great connecting force; love is the way to spiritual development and also the product of spiritual development. The more one becomes conscious of the heart, the better one is able to give and receive more love. The consecratory road to transcending the ego and reconnecting with the whole is 'love in action'. We will discuss several aspects that keep mankind under the illusion. The road to initiation is a path of development on which one realises where one's inner pain is, what that 'pain' is attached to and how one can free oneself from it in order to merge with the Divine once more. By following the road to initiation one rids the ego of all its impeding veils. The ego can then merge consciously with one's higher self. In order to put this into practice, we will suggest exercises to accompany each step below."

Step 1 - You do everything yourself

"We take the first step with the watchword: 'Realise that you do everything yourself'. One of the big illusions in this day and age is that people think they are able to keep everything under control. They think that they are the only ones who can decide what happens in their lives. People often think of themselves as if there were no connection with other people on Earth, with nature, with cosmic phenomena, etc. This is the same as a fish in the Pacific Ocean that imagines itself to be isolated from everything that happens around it; from the tonnes of water in the ocean, from all the millions of fish that swim around it, from the surface of the Earth that is also the ocean floor, from the energy of the sun that keeps the water fluid, from small fish, insects and plankton that are its nourishment, from possible pollution of the seas by man, and from the influence of the moon on the tides and on the behaviour of all that lives in the sea. You must realise the context in which you function. This requires that you shift your focus from your personal circumstances to the whole. By actually doing so in your personal life, you put all sorts of situations, issues and experiences in a different perspective.

Exercise for Step 1 – Putting control into perspective

• Withdraw to a quiet place.

• Breathe deeply into the belly and feel how you relax.

• Evoke a situation in which you thought you had everything under control but things ultimately did not go as you had expected.

• Distance yourself from this situation in your mind.

• Distance yourself some more and become aware of at least three people, aspects or events that influenced the situation.

• Distance yourself some more and become aware of at least three other people, aspects or events that influenced the situation.

• Distance yourself some more and become aware of possibly three more people, aspects or events that influenced the situation.

• View the situation from the outside and become aware of all the different factors that influenced the situation.

• How else can you influence the outcome of the situation other than through control?

• Breathe deeply into the belly and feel how this new possibility feels.

• Accept this possibility in your heart and let it integrate into your life.

• Take your time to experience this.

• Feel your breathing again.

• When you are ready, open your eyes."

Step 2 - Take yourself less seriously

"By taking yourself a little less seriously, you can connect better with the world around you. People are inclined to take themselves much too seriously. Just to be perfectly clear, I would like to make an essential distinction between loving yourself and taking yourself seriously. People nowadays do not have enough love for themselves, they take themselves too seriously and put themselves into perspective too rarely. People live through various dramas in their lives, have little self-confidence and are uncertain about their self-esteem. I mean that people try to compensate a lack of love for themselves through attention, appreciation and respect from others. If matters do not proceed as they had expected, their self-esteem is wounded; they feel passed over or disrespected. People find it difficult to put things into perspective and so can get eternally stuck in 'old' assumptions. The only solution is to return to yourself and to reconnect the love and self-esteem within yourself and let them grow. But be aware, you can only give what you give to yourself. It is a big step on the way to recovery. Being able to be light-hearted and laugh about yourself are characteristics of a freer ego. They are the means for being as uninhibited as a child.

Exercise for Step 2 - Putting being in the right into perspective

• Withdraw to a quiet place.

• Breathe deeply into the belly and feel how you relax.

• Select a situation in which you feel you are in the right, but are not put in the right.

• Become aware of this and evoke the countless times that you have discussed this situation with yourself or with others as the most serious matter in the world.

- Now take a step back, distance yourself from the situation in your mind as if it did not directly concern you but someone else in your position.

- Take another step back and imagine that you are the director of a play in which this drama is taking place and that the various people involved are actors in this play.

- Now transform this drama into a comedy. How do you use the various moments of tension that occur to create comic moments that you and others can laugh about? Do your utmost to make the best possible use of these moments. You have done your utmost if you can laugh about them.

- Take your time to experience this.

- Feel your breathing again.

- When you are ready, open your eyes.

Share this experience with others, so that you can laugh together and enjoy the new perspective."

Step 3 – Forgiving yourself opens the heart

"When I talk about opening the heart, I do not mean the physical heart but the energetic centre of the heart, the heart chakra (see the Glossary) that is situated at the level of the middle of the breastbone. This heart of man is where it is easier for you to become conscious of your own Divine nature by feeling. The heart makes it possible to experience the unity between everything that exists; the more open the heart is, the easier this is."

"Making assumptions, drawing conclusions and acquiring convictions during the course of one's development creates emotional 'pains'. These inner pains do not ensue from the experiences of life but from the interpretation of these experiences. When pain occurs, people choose consciously or unconsciously to close the heart in order to supposedly 'protect' themselves. But it is this 'protection' that causes additional pain and in turn makes it harder to access the heart. This process can only be stopped by deciding to reopen the heart. And this starts by forgiving yourself, by accepting yourself completely and by loving yourself unconditionally. When you forgive yourself you also let go of all sorts of painful habits, attitudes and patterns."

"Forgiving yourself opens your heart and so you can also forgive others and accept them as they are. It opens the way to unconditional love for yourself and for others."

"Forgiving, accepting and being kind create an opening in your consciousness enabling you to experience higher dimensions. This puts you in an upward spiral of growth and development. When your heart opens itself you can connect more consciously with your higher self; your higher self and your soul can then manifest themselves better on Earth and your personality, your human self, becomes more conscious of its Divine nature. And thus you experience more love and compassion in your life."

"To actually open your heart it is important that you become conscious of your negative opinions about yourself and about others. Realise how often you judge and condemn others and yourself every day. Become aware of the cause of these negative opinions and let them go. This is essential for opening the heart."

Exercise 1 for step 3 – To open the heart you need to forgive yourself

"To open the heart you must forgive yourself for everything you hold against yourself.

- Withdraw to a quiet place.

- Make a list of all your aspects/characteristics/deeds/events that you hold against yourself.

- Select the aspect or the characteristic/deed or event that currently demands the most of your attention.

- Breathe deeply into the belly and feel how you relax.

- Connect with the feeling that that aspect or characteristic/deed or event invokes in you.

- Become aware of the physical sensation it causes within you.

- Connect your feeling with your heart (a warm place at the middle of your breastbone).

- Also connect your physical sensation with your heart.

- Become aware of the deep need that is the cause of the aspect or the characteristic/deed or event.

- Connect this need with your heart.

- Declare in your heart:
  'I fully accept the need for ..... in myself.'

- Breathe deeply into the belly and feel how this declaration feels.

- Also declare in your heart:
  'I fully accept this aspect or this characteristic/deed or event ....
  in myself.'

- Breathe deeply into the belly and feel how this declaration feels.

• Declare in your heart:
'I forgive myself for everything that I have held against myself in connection with this aspect or this characteristic/deed or event.'

• Breathe deeply into the belly and feel how this declaration feels.

• Declare in your heart:
'I forgive myself for everything that I have held against myself in connection with the need for/to ......'

• Breathe deeply into the belly and feel how this declaration feels.

• Proceed to the next aspect and apply this exercise to all the aspects on your list.

Exercise 2 for Step 3 – Unconditional acceptance of less positive characteristics

• Make a list of what you see as your positive and less positive characteristics.

• Ask yourself whether these characteristics contain a judgement of yourself or whether it is what others think of you. If the latter is the case, look at the list again to realise that the points were listed by you alone.

• If there are any characteristics you do not want to feel, to which you have a resistance, write them down and list this resistance as a separate characteristic. For example: 'I nibble too much' results in the resistance 'It is not true that I nibble too much'; so the resistance is also a characteristic.

• Accept the possibility that you also have 'less positive' characteristics and feel what this does to you. Breathe deeply into the belly and let this feeling register. You do not have to meet the ideal. That is not what life is all about. Life is about developing the love in your heart; to what extent you are prepared to accept yourself, how conditional or unconditional you are towards yourself, that is the basis. Only when you accept yourself unconditionally can you accept others unconditionally.

• Select a characteristic and say the characteristic to yourself.

• Breathe deeply into the belly and feel how it feels to have this characteristic.

• Let the characteristic enter your heart.

• Is there any resistance to accepting this characteristic?

• If so, breathe deeply into the belly and feel how it feels to have this resistance.

• Proceed to the next characteristic.

• Feel them all one by one and give the extent to which you accept the characteristics a percentage. Use the characteristics that score less than 80% for your next step.

• List your objectionable and also your positive characteristics on various pieces of paper and put them in a bag in order to carry out the following ritual.

• Withdraw to a quiet place so that you can attune to us, Jesus and Mary Magdalene, spiritually without being disturbed.

• Let go of all your prejudiced ideas and assumptions about us before this meeting, which will take place in your inner self. Every assumption about us that evokes fear, worry or distrust can only be false. We stand for love and compassion and it is on this basis that we want to receive you.

- Imagine that you give us your objectionable and your positive characteristics that you have listed on the slips of paper.

- Together we will take a spiritual look at each slip of paper. We fully accept each characteristic you want to give us. Continue until there is nothing left in you. Feel light and free. You do not need to assume a special form. You are everything and nothing. You experience total freedom.

- Imagine that you leave all the characteristics with us and return in peace.

- Take your time to experience this.

- Feel your breathing again.

- When you are ready, open your eyes."

Revelation 16

Jesus and Mary Magdalene discuss the next two steps on the road to the initiation of man on Earth. About 'creating room, emptiness and silence' to come in contact with one's inner self and 'the road of light' with exercises to make people aware of their free will, enable them to make more conscious choices and to focus their attention in order to improve their consciousness. Someone's degree of consciousness determines the extent to which one exercises one's free will.

Step 4 – Creating room, emptiness and silence

Jesus and Mary Magdalene: "People nowadays usually lead a busy life, full of activities and obligations. When you have a bit of spare time you switch on the television or your walkman or you read the newspaper; many of you always have something to do. There is not much time for peace and quiet. Many do not even realise that this is possible. You are always busy stimulating the senses, although you are not aware of doing so. Stimulating the senses is a great diversion. Many people have a certain fear of feeling the emptiness within. When they withdraw and relax they come in contact with their feelings and are confronted with themselves."

"Feeling is the first challenge. The first layer you come across when experiencing peace and quiet is the layer of emotions. This lets you feel how in touch you are with things. And the awakening that goes with this can change someone's life and that is exactly what people are afraid of. If you carry on in peace and quiet, you can encounter an empty feeling. And that is what people are even more afraid of. People have negative feelings about the emptiness, because that is where they encounter the limits of their ego. These are the limits beyond which the ego has nothing to say. This creates an opening for something else; an opening is created for 'the higher self', for the Divine in all people. So the emptiness is a door to higher states of consciousness. At the moment that you come in contact with your own higher self you undergo a transforming experience at the personal level and at the level of the ego. The ego realises that it is an illusion and learns to let go. One becomes freer and happier. Silence is essential in life. There must be room for silence every day because it is an important means for balancing your inner and outer selves. In times like these, people are extremely outwardly oriented and it is necessary for them to come in contact with their inner selves again, so that there can be a balance between their inner and outward selves, between yin and yang, between male and female. We, Jesus and Mary Magdalene, would like to invite you all to make room every day for silence, to release yourselves from obligations, activities, wishes and desires."

Exercise 1 for Step 4 – Prayer as meditation

• Withdraw to a quiet place.

• Close your eyes and take a moment to feel your breathing, deep in your belly.

• Let your body relax and very calmly repeat the Prayer to Christ and/or the Prayer to Mary Magdalene several times. So calmly that you can feel every word. Compare them with the beads on a string; each word is like a bead. Inhale and exhale calmly between each word.

Lord.....Jesus.....Christ.....Son.....of.....God.....have.....mercy....upon .....me....Dear.....Mary.....Magdalene.....Divine.....woman.....Have .....mercy.....upon.....me.....and.....awaken.....in.....me.....Help.....

me.....to.....heal.....and.....appreciate.....the.....female....principle...
within.....me.....In..all.....the.....depths.....of.....my.....being.....
fflin....my.....fellow.....man.....and.....in.....everything.....on.....
Earth.....Amen

- Pause after each prayer and experience the emptiness within yourself. In the silence you may become conscious of inner processes,
of the effect the prayer has on you or of the emptiness within yourself.

Exercise 2 for step 4 – The influence of the prayer on the heart

- Withdraw to a quiet place.

- Close your eyes and take a moment to feel your breathing deep in
your belly.

- Let your body relax and very calmly repeat the Prayer to Christ
and/or the Prayer to Mary Magdalene several times. So calmly that
you can feel every word. Compare them with the beads on a string;
each word is like a bead. Inhale and exhale calmly between each
word.

Lord...Jesus.....Christ.....Son.....of.....God.....have........mercy.....upon
.....me....Dear.....Mary.....Magdalene.....Divine.....woman.....Have...
....mercy.....upon.....me.....and.....awaken.....in.....me.....Help.....me
.....to.....heal.....and.....appreciate.....the....female.....principle.....
within.....me.....In.....all.....the.....depths.....of.....my....being.....in.....
my.....fellow.....man.....and.....in.....everything.....on.....Earth.....
Amen

- Turn your attention to your heart and be still.

- You may notice that after a while you again have other thoughts; this is O.K. Just repeat the prayer and turn your attention back to your heart.

- This cycle will be repeated several times. You will then notice that you relax more and more step by step.

- When you feel you are ready, take a moment to feel your breathing and your body before opening your eyes. It is advisable that you lie down for a few minutes after doing this silence exercise to let the process sink in.

"You may do this silence exercise two times per day, preferably early in the morning or late in the afternoon."

Step 5 – The road of light

"This step can also be called: exercising your own free will or making use of human choices. It is important to realise that people constantly make choices. These choices can be made at various levels of life; at the level of your activities, of your thoughts, of your intentions, of your emotions, of your contact with other people and your association with life in general."

"You constantly make choices at all of these levels. Very often you are not aware of how you do that. Your attention unconsciously turns to things, people and situations that are a repetition of old inner pain. Unconsciously, you often repeat situations that cause the same pain or that compensate your inner pain. You are drawn to the external world. This is done via the senses. And the senses follow the direction of your attention. It is almost an automatic process."

"Giving attention to something has a fostering, constructive effect on the object, on the concept, on the situation, on the people on which you focus your attention. When you become conscious of the process of giving attention you make conscious choices and you become the master of your senses and of your relationship towards the external world, and you create the life you want."

Exercises for Step 5

Exercise 5.1 – Becoming conscious of your attention

• Focus your attention freely on something and become conscious of the choice you make. Also become conscious of your natural tendency not to be conscious of what you focus your attention on.

• To remain conscious of how your attention shifts you can best name each object, idea and aspect and each thought and emotion on which you focus your attention. For instance: candle, cold feeling, the thought of having to do something, a memory of the previous day, not being comfortable in the chair, nice music.

"Do you already have the feeling that you are conscious of your attention? This is a growth process, of course. While focusing your attention, an underlying process is going on inside you and that is the process of experiencing emotions, sensations and states of consciousness. This underlying flow of experiences is linked directly to your attention; it is the source of your attention, but also the effect of your attention. Impulses that guide your attention in a certain direction come from this unconscious level. At the same time, focusing your attention on something has a certain effect on you that influences this flow of experiences, so that you turn your attention in a new direction.

Sometimes you steer your attention to various objects at the same time. For instance: you are doing something and at the same time your thoughts are elsewhere and your body may possibly feel something else, too. You can do all this simultaneously. That's how capable you are.

Exercise 5.2 – Attention focused on various aspects

• Turn your attention freely to something.

• Examine whether you have focused your attention on something else as well. Sometimes on something in the background or on a subtle feeling, almost unconsciously.

• Register all the things on which you focus your attention at the same time and name them.

Repeat this exercise a few times. The exercise is finished when you have gained insight into the way in which you focus your attention on several aspects at the same time.

Exercise 5.3 – Focusing attention on sensations, emotions and changes in consciousness

• Focus your attention freely on something.

• While doing so, become aware of the underlying sensations, emotions or changes of consciousness that occur in you.

• Repeat this exercise until you become aware that these two different phenomena are occurring at the same time.

• Then focus your attention consciously on the sensations, emotions and changes in consciousness.

Repeat this exercise a few times. The exercise is finished when you have gained insight into the way in which your attention and the underlying phenomena occur at the same time."

Exercise 5.4 – Paying specific attention

"You have become conscious of:

A - how you focus your attention and
B - the effect of your attention on your inner self

You are now able to make specific choices. Based on the sensations, emotions and changes in consciousness that you experience, you can choose to focus your attention on the aspects that create the effect you wish to experience. This is your free choice. You can apply your own free will to this. Free will can only exist if you make conscious choices. The extent to which someone is conscious determines the extent to which he or she exercises free will.

• Focus your attention freely on something.

• Become conscious of the underlying sensations, emotions and changes in consciousness.

• On the basis of your sensations, emotions and changes in con- sciousness, decide whether you want to experience them. If so, con- tinue to focus your attention on them. If not, let them go and focus your attention on something else.

Repeat this exercise until you have made ten conscious choices. Note! It may happen that you sometimes wish to experience unplea- sant things, that you want to be angry or sad or want to feel that you are a victim in a certain situation. Realise that this is sometimes a very conscious choice. Also apply the exercises for Step 5 here. Make a note of this experience for yourself."

Revelation 17

Jesus and Mary Magdalene discuss the next three steps on the road to the initiation of man on Earth. About a different view of the function of death as a road to freedom and about opening the heart. By opening the heart, both at an individual and a collective level, Earth becomes a source of enrichment for the Cosmos. The time is ripe for the big transformation, the transformation occurs in the heart. Exercises: 'Each day of your life is a movie', 'We love the Earth' and 'Beliefs about death'.

Step 6 – The road to freedom

Jesus and Mary Magdalene: "There is an invisible process that everybody experiences every day of their lives. People wake up every day and step into a movie, a movie that they have created for themselves with various scenarios and actors. Every day you play your own part in this movie. Every person has created his or her part right down to the last detail. This goes on until you go back to bed and step out of your role, out of the movie, until the next morning. And then it starts all over again. Over the years you have created various scenarios. But nevertheless, it remains your own movie; a very long production that starts at birth and ends in death, with an outing every night. Sometimes, you are so deeply immersed in your own movie that you no longer realise there is so much more in the universe. While sleeping and between death and reincarnation, you can make contact with higher dimensions of existence. You realise deep down that there is more than the movie you step into every day. Incidentally, that is one of the reasons for sleeping: you get away for a while. That is also one of the purposes of dying: to get away for a while. You have played the movie from start to finish; this version of the movie is finished. It is time to refresh yourself."

"During both periods, during sleep as well as after death, you are given the opportunity to digest the processes you experienced in the movie, in your life, which creates room for higher levels of consciousness. Do not think that nothing happens during this interim period. You go through an intensive process of acceptance; a process in preparation of new phases. Deep down, mankind is afraid of these interim periods. This is one reason for insomnia and fear of dying. People are afraid to 'pop off', to lose the familiar frame of reference they are attached to; the illusion of having control. When you can let go of this illusion for a while, you have the opportunity to examine and experience other states of consciousness. You can then also consciously connect your various states of consciousness."

Who am I?

"Integrating the silence exercise into your daily life (see Revelation 16, step 4) is one way to promote this integration. Step by step you realise who you really are. Living in matter on Earth does not mean that that is the only existence. It is only a small part of the whole that you really are. Just as waking and sleeping, reawakening and sleeping again is an ongoing process, death and reincarnation is also a process. Have you ever looked at it in this way? Famous questions: 'Where am I going and where do I come from? Who is the I that I think I am? Is that really me? Or am I something else, am I something more? Am I only on this Earth or am I somewhere else, too, at the same time? Have I met the people I come across in this life before; have I had contact with them before in another life, in another dimension, in an interim period? How does it feel to ask yourself these questions? Let them register. You do not have to answer them straight away. Posing the question is already a force in itself. A broader view is required to give what happens in this life a place and also to put things in perspective. As soon as people realise who they really are, they create an enormous freedom that enables them to be much more light-hearted in experiencing all that happens in this world. Despite their unpleasant experiences, they start to see this world as a big and beautiful playground in which they are allowed to be and play for a while; they feel less attached to what goes on from day to day and can enjoy the moment more. There is no more tension."

Souls are brave

"You often think that people only want to experience what you consider are nice things. However, souls are very curious and brave. When you are not incarnated you view all sorts of earthly experiences impartially from the spiritual world. You then wonder what it would be like to be poor. You are curious as to the intensity of a serious illness. Or you consider it to be a very good opportunity for your development to experience something tragic now and then so that your ego learns to look beyond its own limitations. It is the duty of your soul to become conscious of its Divine nature in an incarnated form. This Divine assignment requires broad experience on Earth that ultimately brings the personality in line with the soul. In practice, this means that in the long run your heart opens completely, that you have complete faith that the Christ-consciousness has awakened in you and that you are ultimately finished with all experiences on Earth. When this is the case you can choose to return to Earth to contribute to the process of other incarnated souls, which in turn is another step in your own evolution."

Everybody is on their own quest

"Have you ever realised how those beliefs about death and the fear of dying impact your life? Have you ever realised how your convictions concerning your relationship with the spiritual world affect you? Have you realised what effect your opinion of your own human nature has on you? It is good that people pay attention to this kind of thing and that they no longer let themselves by carried away by collective beliefs about who we are. Everyone should work that out for themselves. We are there to help. That's what people have our prayers for. Mankind has lost contact with many essential aspects of human life. This has resulted in problems concerning one's relationship with the female principle, with one's own sexuality and with the process of dying. Here is an exercise that will help you experience the immortality of the soul. The journey of the soul through the various lives and through the various days in each life is 'only' a temporary Earthly manifestation of an absolutely immortal soul, an expression of Divine consciousness that wishes to experience life in matter. Many of you still identify strongly with the temporary Earthly manifestation. By means of the following exercise you can clearly experience contact with the Divine essence."

Exercise for step 6 – Experience the immortality of the soul

• Withdraw to a quiet place.

• Close your eyes.

• Breathe deeply into the belly and feel how you relax.

• Visualise a random day in your life as being a movie.

• At the end of the day, when you go to sleep, see and feel how you step out of today's movie.

• There is a short intermission in the movie.

• When you wake up, see and feel how you step back into the movie of this new day.

- What are you going to make of your role today?

- At the end of the day, when you go to sleep, see and feel how you step out of today's movie.

- It is intermission time again.

- When you wake up, see and feel how you step back into the movie of this new day.

- Today is the last day of your life.

- Breathe deeply into the belly and feel how that feels.

- At some time during the day you will die.

- See and feel how you step out of this life's movie.

- Once again, it is intermission.

- See and feel how you step into the movie of a new life when you reincarnate on Earth.

- And this is the first day of this new life.

- What part will you play in this life?

- Breathe deeply into the belly and feel how that feels.

- At the end of the day, when you go to sleep, see and feel how you step out of today's movie.

- It is time for another intermission.

- When you wake up, see and feel how you step back into the movie of this new day.

• And this day is your last day in this life.

• Breathe deeply into the belly and feel how that feels.

• At some time during the day you will die.

• See and feel how you step out of this life's movie.

• In the meantime, it is intermission again.

• See and feel how you step into the movie of a next life when you reincarnate on Earth.

• At the end of this life, when you die, see and feel how you step out of this life's movie.

• And in the meantime, it is intermission.

• See and feel how you step into the movie of a next life when you reincarnate on Earth.

• This is where you are now.

• Distance yourself and look at all the days of the movies of your lives.

• Breathe deeply into the belly and feel how that feels.

• Distance yourself some more and look at all the movies of your various lives with all the intermissions in between.

• Look at the various parts you played.

• Breathe deeply into the belly and feel how that feels.

• Contact the actor who is behind all those parts; that actor is you.

• Breathe deeply into the belly and feel how that feels.

• Take your time to experience this.

• When you are ready, open your eyes.

Step 7 – The way of the heart

"Discovering and accepting one's true nature is an essential step in opening one's heart. The essence of the heart is trust and submission. The counterpart is fear and aggression. As soon as you are afraid, you forget who you really are. No matter what you experience, it can never damage your own Divine essence. This can only occur within the scope of the illusion for which you bear partial responsibility. No one can deprive you of your Divine essence. Nor can you deprive anyone else of theirs. You cannot really damage anyone, even when you murder someone. The illusion that that is possible has kept mankind trapped in an imaginary power game for thousands of years. What a colossal movie! Step out of this movie and try to rebuild your own world from your heart. Your lifestyle, your norms and values, the way in which you associate with each other, will then adjust to the heart. You will then create a beautiful world, a world of love and respect for each other and for all creatures, both on Earth and in the rest of the universe."

"The impact of your actions, of not taking action and of your thoughts is not limited to Earth but reaches other worlds as well; so you also influence other worlds. By opening the heart, both at an individual and a collective level, the Earth becomes a source of enrichment for the Cosmos. It is time for a big transformation. Your relationship with yourself is central in this transformation. The transformation occurs in your own heart. It is a daily process, an ongoing process. Everyone radiates this to their fellow human beings and to their surroundings. Everyone can be a bright spot for the whole."

Exercise for step 7 – We love the Earth

• Withdraw to a quiet place.

• Close your eyes.

• Breathe deeply into the belly and feel how you relax.

• Turn your attention to your heart.

• Feel the love flow from your heart through your body.

• Visualise the Earth as a big ball turning in front of your eyes.

• Send a beam of love from your heart to the centre of the Earth.

• Make contact from your heart with people who are dear to you.

• Visualise these people together with you around the Earth that is turning like a big ball in front of your eyes.

• Send a beam of love all together from your hearts to the centre of the Earth.

• Make contact from your heart with your fellow-countrymen.

• Visualise these people together with you around the Earth that is turning like a big ball in front of your eyes.

• Send a beam of love all together from your hearts to the centre of the Earth.

• Make contact from your heart with all the people on your continent.

• Visualise these people together with you around the Earth that is turning like a big ball in front of your eyes.

- Send a beam of love all together from your hearts to the centre of the Earth.

- Make contact from your heart with all the people who live on Earth.

- Visualise these people together with you around the Earth that is turning like a big ball in front of your eyes.

- Send a beam of love all together from your hearts to the centre of the Earth.

- See and feel how the Earth radiates unconditional love back to you.

- Feel how all of you together merge in unconditional love with the Earth.

Step 8 – Life and death

"The view that a certain culture has of the process of dying determines what level of wisdom that culture can achieve. Cultures that have a fear of dying remain limited to interacting with the material world and are easy to manipulate. Have you ever realised how your fear of dying is constantly fed by the media? Dying or murdering someone, depriving someone of their physical existence is the greatest threat there is, the greatest punishment. Why should this be necessary? Because your relationship with 'death', with 'crossing over' from the material to the spiritual world, can be the very key to freedom. As soon as you are afraid to make contact with other dimensions of existence, you live like 'a dead person' as it were. Actually, being dead has nothing to do with losing the physical dimension. Being dead is, as it were, a life without a heart. But you will have a richer and more lively life if you make contact with your heart and open yourself up to your own spiritual nature. Because you are all spiritual; let there be no misunderstanding in this respect."

Exercise for step 8 – Beliefs about death

• Make a list of all the beliefs you have concerning death, also about your own death.

• Focus your attention on one belief.

• Close your eyes and repeat the belief a few times.

• Breathe deeply into the belly and feel how it feels to have that belief.

• Accept all the emotions that the belief arouses.

• Connect the belief with your heart.

• Make contact between your heart and your higher self (your Divine consciousness) by calling it up: 'Dear higher self, you who are conscious of my Divinity, come into my heart!'

• Become conscious of the immortality of your higher self and of your soul (the link between your higher self and your ego) by asking: 'Dear higher self, you who are conscious of my Divinity, let me experience my immortality.'

• Breathe deeply into the belly and feel how that feels.

• Become conscious of the journey of your higher self and of your soul through your various physical manifestations in the past, present and future by asking: 'Dear higher self, you who are conscious of my Divinity, let me experience my journey through my various physical manifestations in the past, present and future.'

• Feel the freedom that this insight gives.

• Accept your own immortality.

- Feel your immortality in your heart.

- Let this feeling spread over your entire body.

- When you die your physical body will be taken over by Mother Earth with complete love.

- Breathe deeply into the belly and feel how that feels.

- Feel the love of Mother Earth flow through your entire body.

- Feel the connection with Mother Earth in your heart and open yourself to her love.

- Become aware that your higher self and your soul organise all the elements that Mother Earth lends your body according to their own consciousness.

- Breathe deeply into the belly and feel how that feels.

- You may give your body permission to reunite with Mother Earth when it can no longer be of service.

- Breathe deeply into the belly and feel how that feels.

- You may thank your body for everything it did, does and will do for you while you are allowed to be together.

- Breathe deeply into the belly and feel how that feels.

- Take a moment to return to your physical reality.

"Apply the exercise once to each belief. You can run through your list over a longer period of time."

Revelation 18

Jesus and Mary Magdalene discuss the ninth step on the road to the initiation of man on Earth. On preparing for death and the assistance of the spiritual world in this preparation, the transformation of consciousness on the way through the tunnel to the immaterial world and the development process that takes place there. Exercise to experience the process of dying.

Step 9 – The process of dying

Jesus and Mary Magdalene: "As we already mentioned previously, one of the main factors that can open people's hearts is integrating the process of dying in everyone's life. We will now take you by the hand to go through this process together."

Preparing for death

"To start, we would like to say that no one is ever alone when they are in the process of dying. That process already starts before one stops breathing or before the last heart beat. It already starts a few days before that. The people involved are prepared by us, or by other guides if their souls are better attuned to them. At a certain stage we approach them on a spiritual level to announce what will happen. We let them explore the experience of dying and feel the love of the spiritual world while they are sleeping or when they are in a deep state of rest. Some people are more conscious of these experiences than others. Some even see us. Others feel us, consciously or unconsciously. Some experience a new deep calm that helps them let go of their attachment to life, to those they hold dear, to their possessions. We help them take their leave and prepare for their journey. It is a time of much spiritual activity. We also take care of their dear ones, their process of acceptance, so that they too can let their loved ones go. We accompany the dying to the gate of death. They must pass this themselves to enter the tunnel towards the light. We are there for them at a distance. But they must step out of life themselves. In the same way as they stepped into life. We will come back to this in Revelation 19."

To the light through death

"Imagine that you are at the entrance to the tunnel towards the light, ready to leave everything behind you. This is a special moment of which you have dreamt or fantasised on occasion. It is the ultimate experience of letting go, of surrendering completely. If you can let yourself go, dying is a mild process through which you release yourself from the material, through which you take leave of the physical body. You are pulled along, as it were, in the process. By really detaching yourself from life you can experience the process of dying with a feeling of joy and also of freedom; you can experience it as an awakening and see the truth of existence."

"The process of dying has contractions, just like the process of birth. During birth, during passage through the mother's birth canal as one becomes restricted by the body, the consciousness narrows. While dying, during passage through the gate and the tunnel towards the light, the consciousness is expanded. We are on the other side of the tunnel waiting to receive you. In the tunnel you experience a profound encounter with yourself. You discover yourself in all the depths of your 'being'."

"You have prepared yourself for this encounter with yourself all your life. The outcome of the process that you undergo in the tunnel determines your process in the other dimension. You then experience various transformation processes. After the tunnel you need to recover and you are still very occupied with yourself, with your own spirit and with recognising where you are, what is going on. After this transitional process you can make contact with us and with relatives, old friends and acquaintances who died before you. And often you will also want to make contact with the world you have left. This can be very confronting, but in the end it also helps you accept the process of dying and your new situation. You may experience that contact for a moment in your own way, but then you go on. There is plenty to do in this other world as well. You receive from us a kind of emotional and mental support and spiritual guidance that precisely fits your level of consciousness. You first go through a period of isolation and of withdrawing into yourself. And you get to see and experience your whole life all over again. This takes place in a kind of energetic egg. When difficult or unresolved moments in your life on Earth present themselves, guides help you to resolve these moments so that you can detach yourself from them. Energy is released during this process of disengagement, making you feel lighter. You also acquire new understanding at various levels. After you have come to terms with your life, you start to open yourself and you are able to connect with this apparently new world. At that moment you may express a wish. Where would you like to go? What is your deepest spiritual wish?"

"Based on this wish, you start to participate in a certain process of awareness. You are placed under the guidance of guides whose development is more advanced than yours and you are given a kind of training. The more your wishes are geared to unconditional love, the more you may participate in pure levels of the light. We advise you to attune yourself at that moment to what is the highest and most loving within yourself. And especially to focus on the light. When you have united with the light and have surrendered to the light, you may participate in guiding people on Earth or in other tasks that are specifically meant for you."

Closer and closer to the Divine

"As you develop further, you can make contact with guides and souls who are on a higher level of development and who have greater responsibilities in 'the other world', such as guiding various animal species and the harmony between them, harmonising the plant world with the animal world on Earth and ultimately contacting and guiding life on other planets. When you are ready, you may undergo student placement, as it were, in these various processes. And what we mean by 'when you are ready' is that you have left your personal interests behind you and are able to surrender to the greater cosmic whole. In this way you get closer and closer to the Divine. The period of time between dying and reincarnating is very much determined by your most profound spiritual wishes that bring you into a new development process in the immaterial world. At a certain point you may also be confronted with the possibility of being born again. You can opt for this rebirth or you can decide to remain in the spiritual world for a while longer. There are souls that long so much for the material life that they are quickly attracted to being reincarnated, yet they must first complete a process of acceptance in the spiritual world."

Exercise for step 9 – Experience the process of dying

"With this exercise you can go through a process of dying and become conscious of the immortality of your consciousness. This exercise can only be done in the presence of someone else; one person slowly reads the exercise out loud while the other does the exercise. The person who does the exercise must indicate to the other person at the beginning of the exercise the speed that he or she feels is good for doing the exercise. Agree on a code to make it easy for you to indicate that more time is required for a certain step or that you are ready. Should you wish to interrupt the exercise, indicate this to your assistant and follow the instructions at the end of the exercise to 'return to the here and now'.

- Withdraw to a quiet place.

- Close your eyes and turn your attention to your breathing.

- Breathe deeply into the belly and feel how you relax.

- Imagine you are dying.

- You have had a fulfilling life and you prepare yourself to leave this world.

- You have taken your leave of everything and everyone dear to you.

- You have transferred all your earthly affairs and left them behind you.

- You feel free and unattached.

- You are relaxed and you experience the process with complete acceptance.

- You are in your heart and you surrender to this special experience.

- You feel that your consciousness is slowly withdrawing from your physical body.

- Your physical senses pass on less and less information.

- Your attention withdraws into your heart.

- You feel much love and trust in your heart.

- You feel you are being carried.

- You are completely enveloped by Divine love.

- You feel the presence and the loving guidance of your guides towards the light.

- The time has come to step out of your physical body.

- You exhale for the last time.

- You feel your physical heart stop.

- You become aware of your own consciousness that is separate from your physical body.

- You slowly let go of your physical body.

- You feel your consciousness become lighter and freer.

- You also let go of your identities in this life, of your personality, of your ego.

- You feel your consciousness become even lighter and freer.

- You are now at the gate, ready to permanently leave this life.

- You go through the gate.

- You connect with your own Divinity, with your own light, with your own love.
  Take all the time you need to experience this.

- You enter the tunnel of light and love.

- You connect with your own Divinity, with your own light, with your own love.
  Take all the time you need to experience this.

- You proceed and are born in this other dimension; you are welcomed.

- Who are waiting for you? Do you see your guides, angels, relatives, old friends and loved ones? Take all the time you need to experience this.

- You feel the immortality of your consciousness. Take all the time you need to experience this.

- You concentrate on the highest level of light and Divine love. Take all the time you need to experience this.

- Slowly make contact again with your breathing and with your body.

- Feel your hands and feet and move them slowly until you feel you are back in your body.

- Take a few minutes and when you are ready, slowly open your eyes.

- Take another moment for yourself to return to the here and now (your assistant will remind you of the date and the place where you are now).

- Drink something warm to feel you are back in your body.

- If it makes you feel good, you can share your experience with your assistant.

If you want to exchange places and the assistant wants to be assisted, it is better not to do this immediately after this first session. It is advisable to wait several hours between the two sessions or to do the second session the following day."

What happens in the case of 'unnatural' death?

"People who have a fatal accident are prepared for this too at the level of their soul some time in advance. Their loved ones have also been able to adjust to this beforehand. This takes place unconsciously, for instance while sleeping. For evolutionary reasons, the soul has taken the decision to step out of the world prematurely. This step can have been prepared even before birth, but can also have manifested itself in the course of that person's life as a good option for the evolution of the soul. So accidents are never something unexpected at the level of the soul, as people often think. The personality of the person is usually not really aware of it, but the soul guides the person during the process and makes sure that everything goes according to plan."

"In the case of collective accidents or military strikes, the souls of the victims involved had already volunteered to participate in a certain collective process that will accelerate both their personal evolution and the evolution of mankind. Agreements on this are made at the level of the soul. This may be confusing for family and friends, but they too are assisted in this difficult process by their higher selves and by the White Brother- and Sisterhood. And no matter how unreal this may sound to many people, they too have made agreements at the level of the soul to experience the loss of a loved one and the ensuing process of mourning."

"All the prayers contained in this book are a good means for those who remain behind to find consolation and to gain insight into their own experience and into the road the deceased has taken. The people who gave up their lives in the United States on 11 September 2001, for instance, dedicated themselves, together with the Afghans who were killed during the retaliatory action, to a lasting change on Earth and especially to showing mankind that opening the heart is an urgent and vital process. These souls know that love must become the dominant power on Earth. That's what they stand for. Their own hearts were opened to a great extent by their effort and they feel closely connected, from the spiritual world, to all of mankind and Earth."

And what happens in case of murder?

"Here, too, the soul is involved beforehand in the tragic event, but by way of distinction, in the case of a murder there is always a karmic relationship between the murderer and the murder victim. There are various possibilities:

1 – There is an impossible love. Two souls who would like to experience unity together are unable to accomplish this lovingly. The murder ensures that they remain connected so that they can meet each other with love in a next life or evolutionary stage, can forgive each other and so ultimately let each other go.

2 – The murder victim devotes him- or herself to the evolution of the murderer and/or vice versa. Both develop themselves through this event. This does not mean that it is an easy process. Its effect, which is supervised by light beings if requested, is intense and often painful. It is surprising to both parties to discover that it is impossible to actually deprive the other of his or her existence, that there is actually no such thing as death."

And in case of suicide?

"In case of suicide, the person involved desperately tried to make contact with his or her heart, but was unsuccessful due to his or her negative self-image. The suicide is also guided by his or her guardian angels during and after this act of despair. The person will first need to forgive him- or herself before being allowed to reincarnate. In the spiritual world, he or she is admitted to the department of 'intensive care for death aftercare'. His or her guides and helpers decide in mutual consultation when this soul is again ready for a stay on Earth."

Revelation 19

Jesus and Mary Magdalene discuss the tenth step on the road to the initiation of man on Earth. Which process does the soul go through before it reincarnates in the material world? The soul can choose one of three lives. The soul chooses its new parents and brings about a lifelong commitment of the heart. Exercise to become conscious of your own conception. Every child is wanted.

Step 10 – The rebirth

Jesus and Mary Magdalene: "People may wonder what brings them back to Earth if they have died and are in the spiritual world. How does this work? We will explain. When you have exhausted your previous life you are given the opportunity to enter into various areas of consciousness. Your degree of consciousness determines what you are ready for. Your spirit can enter new spiritual areas in the immaterial world, from where you can develop yourself further. If you are not yet ready for this, you need a new incarnation on Earth to take further steps in your individual development process. The Earth, incidentally, is not the only planet on which one can incarnate."

Passing or not passing through the gate

"Preparing for a new birth is also a spiritual development process. It means you must be prepared to let go of the old identity you had during your previous life on Earth. And that, too, is a certain kind of dying.
Some would like to reincarnate quickly. Others decide to continue their spiritual process in the immaterial world. For a new life on

Earth you pass through a gate before incarnating that ensures that you lose your old identity. You can only pass through this gate if you are actually able to throw off your old identity. The key to this gate is your ability to detach yourself from your ego and to accept yourself and others unconditionally. To be able to do this your heart must be above your mind in your consciousness. Only then are you able to pass through this gate. You can also get the urge to reincarnate on Earth at a later point in time in your development process. If you cannot pass through the gate, this does not mean by definition that you will not incarnate on Earth again. There is a middle course. You can take new tasks upon yourself at your current level of consciousness in the immaterial world, such as welcoming those who have recently died and assisting the guides of those who incarnate. These tasks advance you in your development so that at some stage you will be able to pass through the gate and still incarnate. And even then you can still choose to fulfil your current tasks for a while longer. Your stay in this zone does, however, have its limits. For your development you will eventually need to decide on a change. You cannot remain on the same level 'forever'."

Three options for incarnation

"As soon as you have chosen the path of incarnation, you are assisted in and prepared for this in a special way. There are special spiritual guides who carry out this task. You are also prepared for letting go of your ego. Unresolved and unconscious aspects of the ego, which is also referred to as karma, can be worked out in your next life on Earth. In this way you are also prepared for being able to function again in a dimension with time and space. This mainly takes place in the womb during pregnancy, but a basis is also laid for this prior to conception. When you are ready, you are presented with a selection of possibilities for where and when you can incarnate. There are usually three options with various circumstances. One of these three options will appeal to you most strongly and you centre on it as if 'by nature'."

Energetic umbilical cord

"When confronted with these options for a new life on Earth, you experience an energetic composition of the family in which you can be born, the state of consciousness of the parents and relatives and the potential opportunities that that life holds for you and that can be worked out further in the course of your life. During this confrontation, you have the opportunity of saying 'yes' or 'no'. If you say 'no', you distance yourself from this opportunity and one of the other two options may possibly be considered, but in most cases you will return to the middle area where you work out this process further until you are again able to assume certain tasks in this zone. The process you go through in this case is similar to the acceptance process of souls that have experienced a miscarriage."

"If you say 'yes', you experience a connection with your future parents that assumes the form of an energetic umbilical cord that joins with the womb of the woman and the genitals of the man and thus forms the energetic basis for the conception. From the consciousness of your heart, a union is created with the heart of the woman and the heart of the man, your future parents. The union of the heart between the three of you (child and parents) remains present during your entire life."

Exercise for step 10 – The conception

"This exercise will help you to become conscious of the choice of your moment of birth and to take responsibility for it.

• Withdraw to a quiet place.

• Close your eyes and turn your attention to your breathing.

• Breathe deeply into the belly and feel how you relax.

- Turn your attention back in time to the moment before you were conceived in this life. You are still a soul in the presence of your possible future parents. They are being intimate with each other, but have not yet conceived you.

- Feel how it feels to be there with them, how they make you feel.

- Feel how you feel, how your consciousness is at that moment.

- Feel how your potential mother feels, how her consciousness is at that moment.

- Feel how your potential father feels, how his consciousness is at that moment.

- Feel how your potential parents feel with each other, how their relationship is at that moment.

- Feel the attraction that draws you to these people and recognise what it is exactly that appeals to you so that you want to be born of them.

- Feel how you fit in this family.

- Feel how this family fits you.

- Become aware of the circumstances that these parents can offer you: the social circumstances and financial situation of the parents, the brothers and sisters born before you, possible brothers and sisters to be born after you, other relevant relatives, the country they live in, the time in history, the political situation in the country in which you can be born, etc. Explore all the details of your possible birth.

- Recognise the possibilities these parents and these circumstances can offer you.

• Feel whether your potential mother is open to you; does she want and does she have room for a child? Is she prepared to take care of you? What can she mean to you?

• What can you mean to her?

• Does she say 'yes' to you?

• Do you say 'yes' to her?

• Feel whether your potential father is open to you; does he want and does he have room for a child? Is he prepared to take care of you? What can he mean to you?

• What can you mean to him?

• Does he say 'yes' to you?

• Do you say 'yes' to him?

• Once you have said 'yes' to each other, you have chosen each other and you may be conceived.

• Notice how your spiritual hearts connect and feel how that feels.

• Notice how the energetic connections prior to conception are established between you and feel how that feels.

• Open yourself from your heart to experience everything you can experience in this life. Take your time to enjoy it.

• Breathe deeply into the belly and make contact again with your body.

• Slowly open your eyes and return to the here and now."

But what if the child is not welcome?

"There will be people who say that the previous exercise is no use because they think they were unwelcome as a baby. However, a child is never unwanted. Even if the personality of the parents is not geared to the birth of the child, the people involved have always said 'yes' at the level of the soul. You see, at the level of the soul no experience is ever forced on someone if it is not wanted. For certain reasons, the soul said 'yes'. The relevant parents may turn against the decision of the soul at the level of their personality after the birth, but that is exactly the 'game' they created for themselves in order to work it out in accordance with the Divine plan and take a step in their evolution. In the end, the parents actually did take action to enable the birth and the child's soul did decide to be conceived by those parents, to not cause a miscarriage, to want to live on and to be born. The child had nine months to withdraw in the form of a miscarriage. Sometimes this is meant to happen for the development of all people concerned. Your vision of death, which is limited from your earthly perspective, makes your feelings about such a special experience so grievous and this is why there is often little room for forgiveness and parting with love. Feelings of guilt about miscarriages or abortions can keep people in pain for years, which delays the opening of the heart. Forgiving yourself and the foetus is an essential healing for this event."

"In the case of a rape, the above-mentioned factors also play a part. For certain reasons, the mother accepts the birth of the child and the soul of the child also agrees to this option. There are various reasons for wanting such an experience. For instance, the child's wish to heal the mother's pain. It may be that the child was a rapist in a former life and now wants to be there with love for the woman who was raped. But there can be a whole range of other reasons, such as that the child hates men, the child is convinced that love between men and women is impossible or the child explicitly wants to experience, in this life, what it is like to grow up without a father. But in all these cases, all the people involved agreed to the arrival of the child at the level of the soul. Ultimately, therefore, no one is unwanted on Earth. No birth, no matter what the circumstances, is by chance and every birth serves a higher purpose."

Revelation 20

Jesus explains the true meaning of the crucifixion and how
he was called to it. He did not die for our sins. Being nailed
to the cross was a initiation for the human heart at a level
that was as yet unknown to mankind. And the Earth was
initiated into a higher state of consciousness that was and is
unique in its own history and that of the entire Cosmos.
Prayer and exercises to awaken the Christ-consciousness in
the heart.

Jesus: "I would like to share something intimate with you.
Something I experienced myself. It is an event that took place on
various levels. You know certain aspects of the story of the crucifixion, but the essence of this ritual is the inner process that has
occurred and still occurs in every person as a result of the crucifixion. The crucifixion also influenced the collective process that
took place on Earth. My crucifixion was also a initiation of the Earth.
This ritual placed the Earth in another vibration, enabling it to take
a step up in its position in the cosmic order. The Earth too is a being
that is evolving and has an interactive and multidimensional relationship with other planets, stars and solar systems."

"While I was nailed to the cross a connection was made between a
source of unconditional love in the universe and the centre of the
Earth. I was used as an antenna to realise that connection. The Earth
continues to radiate that energy from its core to all creatures that live
on it. The Earth was initiated at that time into a higher state of consciousness that is unique in its history and that is also unique in the
Cosmos. It was an opening for a new universal order whose meaning was to return the people to their source, to reconnect them with

their own essence. People had largely forgotten this connection during the process they went through to exercise their free will on Earth. Extraterrestrial powers and beings were also involved in this process; they too wanted to experience, for instance, what it was like to exercise personal power. All this placed Mother Earth in a downward spiral so that she could no longer offer safety to the creatures for which she provides a home. She felt torn because as a mother she could not care for her children properly. She asked God for help. Many people also prayed for a transformation. The cosmic order was good and conducive to changes. An impulse to start this transformation came from the purest level of the Divine. I volunteered and was chosen as the bearer of the Christ-energy, the higher expression of Divine love and compassion. Mary Magdalene was also chosen with me to bear the Christ-energy, but her task did not include being crucified. The descent of such a pure impulse from the highest level of the Divine onto a planet was a unique event in the entire Cosmos."

The crucifixion was a initiation for the heart

"Through this descent of the Christ-energy, the Earth was returned to a loving vibration that it had lost after the loss of the continent of Atlantis, but this time at a much higher and purer level; a level that the Earth did not as yet know. The same thing happened to the people, at both a collective and an individual level. The crucifixion was a initiation for the human heart in a way that was new to mankind. There had been times before that in which the people experienced a higher state of consciousness. But in terms of evolution they had not yet gone through the deepest abyss. They still had to experience something, namely the need to exercise personal power. This experience closed their hearts and led them far away from the consciousness of their own Divinity. And that entailed much pain, guilt and 'emptiness'. This is the supreme experience of the third dimension, being in matter on Earth. However, this painful experience also brought with it something very positive, namely the human longing for the Divine. And that is what opened the way for the Christ-energy on Earth. People have a thirst for love and the Christ-energy is the source that can quench this thirst. This source lies in everyone's heart."

"It is unique that mankind has incarnated on Earth, has descended into matter, has alienated itself from the Divine, only to return consciously to this source. By incarnating and fully undergoing the human process on Earth, people could explore in detail what it is like to function in matter. This made them more mature and better able to understand the Divine aspect. They now have the experience that enables them to choose between ego and power on the one hand and Divine love on the other hand. To be sure, the ego is also a manifestation of the Divine, but it gives people the illusion of isolation and that makes them lose the connection with the whole. However, they must experience this until they are finished with it."

"At the moment that I was allowed to bring the Christ-energy onto Earth, enough awareness had, however, been created to make this possible. My arrival was not requested by planet Earth alone, but also by various groups on Earth, such as the Essenes, 'Wisemen from the East', Native People and various other groups in all sorts of cultures on Earth. Furthermore, various extraterrestrial beings that are involved in the development of the Earth also requested my arrival."

Jesus did not die for our sins

"What happened to you then? Every person who was incarnated on Earth at the time of the crucifixion underwent a initiation, whether consciously or unconsciously. A very pure aspect of the human heart and of the sixth chakra (see the Glossary) was activated. Like a ray of light that falls on a diamond. The light radiated from their hearts through to the other chakras, the other energy centres in the human body. The vibration of the heart induced in each of them a memory of being Divine, either consciously or unconsciously. This vibration was later passed on to subsequent generations so that the souls that were not incarnated at that time could still experience it physically at a later date. This initiation permanently changed history on Earth because it again placed people in an upward spiral as regards their consciousness; it had its ups and downs, but the movement was and is nevertheless undeniable. The opening of the human heart manifested itself on a social level as well."

"The idea that I died to bear humanity's 'sins' is thus a mistaken, guilt-laden human interpretation of a great cosmic event that had a different purpose. It was a initiation of mankind, of the Earth and of myself as the bearer of the Christ-energy. This Divine essence has always been in mankind but you could no longer connect with it due to your reduced consciousness. The crucifixion activated the Christ-energy within mankind and this enabled you to realise that you are creators and Divine. So that you could also connect with souls that are on a higher level of development, such as the White Brother- and Sisterhood."

There is no such thing as sin

"In this connection it is important for mankind to know that sin, as people interpret this term, does not exist. You do, however, have inner pain as a result of your blinding and estrangement from your true nature. The consciousness of many of you does not fit in with being a Divine being; rather, it corresponds with the division between the Divine and the material that is in your minds. Inner pain and an unfulfilled feeling occur when people cannot unite the Divine and the material with each other. You then look for fulfilment in the material. There is nothing wrong with this, but that fulfilment is only temporary."

"The duality of good and evil can also be very relative in this case. Sometimes it is not always clear what is good and what is evil. From a human point of view it is often a matter of personal interpretation.

What one person considers to be good can be entirely wrong in someone else's opinion. So there are individual and collective 'quests' for mankind on Earth that have turned into abuses and are 'forbidden' in the Ten Commandments, but these people still need these experiences or think they need them in order to learn by bitter experience. The Ten Commandments are essentially restrictions on the ego's possibility to experience things and thus they contribute to opening the human heart, provided they are observed. People can experience pain if they wish, but the Ten Commandments advise against certain essential types of pain. Taking the Divine advice seriously and acting upon it is a personal decision. People sometimes ignore the Divine advice, consciously or unconsciously, and prefer to experiment and experience things in order to learn to distinguish the good and the evil in themselves; in order not to deny the evil in themselves but instead to acknowledge it, give it a place, in order to deal with it consciously so that they can transform and transcend it."

"However, there are other forms of damage or estrangement as well that you, oddly enough, often find acceptable and consider to be 'good', but that also involve pain, such as slaughtering animals, the financial and political suppression of countries, speculating and ma-nipulating with money, discriminating minority groups, destroying nature, waging war, etc., etc. What are your criteria for 'good' and 'evil'? When you hurt yourself and others, you injure your heart and those of the others. And this is an entirely different interpretation of the word 'sin'. There is something else above good and evil and that has to do with love, compassion and honesty. Becoming aware that you have both something good and evil in yourself makes you com-passionate and forgiving. And that is what awakens the Christ-consciousness in your heart."

Transforming duality in thinking

"People are better able to connect with others and the world when they get to know themselves better, love themselves and see themselves in perspective. It is therefore also important for human transformation that people gain insight into the phenomenon of duality, a term that is used regularly in this book. I will explain. When you are awake you are in a certain state of consciousness. This state becomes the most explicit by dividing all your experiences in two poles, two extremes; this can be called duality. The strongest polarisation emerges in situations that you label as being 'welcome' and 'unwelcome'. These qualifications correspond with your idea of 'good' and 'evil'. Your basic attitude and way of thinking is that you organise your lives according to what you consider to be welcome and good and you turn away from what you consider to be unwelcome and evil. This is the level of consciousness on which your personality functions. However, the soul functions in a higher state of consciousness where good and evil do not exist as extremes. Wanting to integrate the experience of good and evil boosts you to a higher level of consciousness and makes you attune yourself to your soul and understand at a deeper level who you are. If you constantly move between two poles in your life and often see things as being either black or white, it is usually difficult to understand and work out unwelcome experiences. However, at a certain moment during your evolution, you will realise otherwise and free yourself from the illusion of dual thinking in order to become a person who sees things more in perspective and who experiences a consciousness of unity."

The crucifixion activated the Christ-consciousness in everyone's heart

"From the moment that the Romans arrested me in the Garden of Gethsemane until my ascension I served as an important example for you, an example of your own Divinity. I wanted to show you who you really are and that there is basically no difference between you and me. The difference between us is that you are still not aware of your true identity and I am. That is why I was nailed to the cross as an example for you. Not that you have to be crucified, but it is necessary that you learn to listen to your own heart and learn to accept and integrate your own Divinity just like I did. So I did not die on the cross for your sins, because sins do not exist in the eyes of God. In your search for wellbeing on Earth you make what are 'mistakes' from a human point of view that usually result in a guilty conscience but that in fact contain useful elements on your evolutionary path of personal development. In your own deliberations, in what you think and what you do, it is nevertheless best to follow your heart. I can show you the way in this respect, but it is up to you to follow or not. When I was nailed to the cross your hearts were moved, together with the Earth, and the latent Christ-consciousness that was within you and in the Earth was activated. My crucifixion activated the Christ-consciousness in your hearts. This is a course that you must follow yourself. You must opt for this yourself; I cannot do that for you. But I can support you in this choice and you can always pray to me."

The crucifixion was Jesus' initiation

"For me, the crucifixion was a initiation, a complete surrender to God, to the Divine. I had to let everything go, which I did in Gethsemane. After that I was ready for it. With every step on the Way of the Cross I let go of part of my ego and before the moment of my death I had completely surrendered myself to God. The aggression of the soldiers and of the people symbolises the fear and aggression that all people direct at their own hearts. So the crucifixion mirrors an inner process that occurs in your own consciousness; you resist your own essence, love and power. You crucify yourself every day with the inner pains that you bring upon yourself. The complete surrender to your own heart and Divinity is the solution to these pains."

"I was nailed to the cross for one day, but you actually nail yourselves to the cross your entire life until you forgive yourselves and accept your own Divine essence and manifestation. I am not the one to forgive you, you must do that yourself. You can forgive yourselves and I will support you in this and show you the way. But forgiveness must come from your own heart. It is your own accusations that cause you to live in pain, fear, aggression and guilt. Guilt forms a heavy shroud that hangs over the Earth. Free yourself and the Earth by forgiving yourself for your 'mistakes' and living from the heart."

"As for myself, the honour and the blessing of being allowed to pass on the Christ-energy to the Earth and to mankind has had a tremendous influence on my spiritual development. I have been given access to levels of love and unity that were unknown to me before. All possible individual aspects of my ego were permanently merged into the ecstasy of the Divine. This is an experience that is latently present in every person and that becomes manifest for everyone at the right moment. You can make contact with the Christ-energy by saying the following prayer.

Dear Christ
Who is present in my heart
Awaken in me
And through me
In everything that exists
Amen

Exercise 1 – Arousing the Christ-consciousness in the heart

• Withdraw to a quiet place.

• Close your eyes and turn your attention to your breathing.

• Breathe deeply into the belly and feel how you relax.

• Turn your attention to everything that you like about yourself. Open yourself and take your time to explore and experience it and to feel how it feels.

- Turn your attention to everything you do not like about yourself. Open yourself and take your time to explore and experience it and to feel how it feels.

- Be aware that both good and evil are in you and that they are a unity.

- Embrace them in your heart with compassion.

- Let the Christ-consciousness awaken in your heart. Say out loud: 'The Christ-consciousness in my heart is awake!'

- Experience the unconditional love of your Christ-consciousness.

- Let your good and your evil sides dissolve in the unconditional love of your Christ-consciousness.

- Enjoy it.

- Breathe deeply into the belly and make contact again with your body.

- Slowly open your eyes and return to the here and now."

Exercise 2 –The repetitive power of the mantra

"You can also use the sentence: *'The Christ-consciousness in my heart is awake!'* as a mantra. A mantra is a word or a sentence with a special spiritual power. By repeating it to yourself, the effect of this sentence goes deeply into your heart and into all the levels of your consciousness.

You can repeat the sentence during your normal day-to-day activities but also during a moment of rest, of course. In both cases you must turn your attention to your heart.

• Breathe deeply into the belly and feel how you relax.

• Repeat the sentence *'The Christ-consciousness in my heart is awake!'* several times in your heart.

• Let the sentence register."

Revelation 21

In the course of the years to come, more and more people will move out of the cities in pursuit of peace and quiet and the nature of the countryside; this to escape from the head and into the heart. The spiritual masters unfold their plans for new residential and working communities called the 'Christ Project'. The plans are centred on spiritual values and an environmentally friendly economy. Exercise for the integration of all people and other forms of consciousness to create a network of love and light.

Mary, Jesus and Mary Magdalene: "There are certain places on Earth that function as entrances for higher energies. These places have a special electromagnetic composition and a certain connection with the Cosmos, which makes it easier to connect the Earth with other dimensions. These places have also been the basis for various civilisations on Earth or for momentous and sometimes heated social processes. The people who live in these areas experience certain energies or fields of force that they are not always able to define. Recollections of these phenomena are often found in popular traditions. Examples of these places are Jerusalem, the Middle East in general, Hawaii, the Bermuda triangle, the Andes mountain range, the Himalayas, the North and South Poles and certain areas in Siberia and Australia."

"These places have something special to offer. The people undergo certain experiences and initiations there. In some cases it can be favourable to live and work in these places; other areas can be almost too intense. There are also certain energetic places that are highly suitable for building a new world; places that almost automatically attract light."

"Over the next ten years, mankind will undergo certain profound processes that will lead to major developments on Earth. People will seek out the countryside, naturally and spontaneously. People will gradually withdraw from the stress and tension of the large cities. Large cities cause one to act too much 'from the head'. There one is distracted by consuming, nourishing one's own ego and attaining power. In the course of the years to come you will be drawn more to the countryside, because there it is easier to come into your heart and you feel more 'at home'. The peace and quiet that the countryside provides helps people to find themselves again. And these conditions will inspire people to create small settlements that are linked together in the form of a network with a centre from where joint activities can be undertaken, such as trade and banking."

"By becoming more a part of nature, mankind will acquire better access to the mysteries of the Earth and the mysteries of its own history. The Earth has much to tell for those who wish to listen. This process would be the reverse of what is happening now. Mankind is currently in a process of concentration of power, of alienation in matter, and in certain respects it has 'gone astray'. To reverse this development people must let something go, namely the need for power and dominance. Only then will other qualities of the human essence manifest themselves, only then will mankind acquire access to other states of consciousness and other dimensions and be able to connect consciously with the Cosmos."

A responsible economy

"Settling in more natural surroundings can easily be combined with a natural form of prosperity. Production is turned in an increasingly sound direction. Quality and ecological protection become important preconditions for industrial production. The new economy is run purely on an environmentally friendly basis. We invite mankind to start up such a project, a society in miniature. This project can show the rest of the world that by living from the heart one can be environmentally friendly and successful at the same time. The social values that go with it will be aimed at creating an ideal society. The buildings will also be constructed according to the laws of nature. The people who live there will experience prosperity and happiness. Such a community is profoundly connected with the Earth and the Cosmos. In the course of time, various projects with the same intentions but with local touches will commence in the world. These various initiatives will be linked to each other and collaborate closely. They will function as a network of the light, gradually priming a completely new economy. The people will be increasingly attracted to these kinds of projects, thereby bringing about a reversal in the world's social structure and economic policy. The great rulers of today will have little say there because the interests there are quite different from those of contemporary society. In this new context it will be easier for mankind to connect with Divine powers and with the network of the light that collaborates with mankind from other dimensions."

A place for transformation

"The project as mentioned above will not be implemented as a reaction to contemporary society, but as a movement that functions alongside contemporary society. The goal of the new economy is not to conflict with the current order, but to take steps forward. The new concept is enriching and inspiring. Spirituality and spiritual norms and values are pivotal. Everything that is conducive to personal development, human relations and love in society is given a prominent role. At this moment there are many people on earth who are ready for such a change; they experience this in the form of personal crises in relationships, at work or at a spiritual level. What is actually happening is that these people are ready for a profound change and they feel that this is difficult to realise in the current order. Many people are attracted to such a project. There are also souls who want to be born into this new order. They are waiting for these bright spots to be created. They are old and developed souls who want to bring a new message. The final transformation of mankind, allowing the higher self to incarnate completely and to awaken the Christ in the human heart, is possible under these conditions. Although these are not the only conditions under which the latter can occur, they are conditions that make this process possible on a collective level. They ensure that changes in the aura of mankind will actually manifest themselves, enabling the entire planet to rise to a higher level of consciousness."

The basis for the Christ Project

"The funds required for starting up such a project must be donated on an entirely altruistic basis and may in no way tarnish the policy and the purity of this project. Those who invest must do so from the heart with the intention of building a new world and not with the intention to exercise personal power or to reserve a privileged position for themselves. No existing organisation may dominate this project or claim it only for itself. They may be involved and contribute, but they must be prepared to function on a universal basis."

"A board of directors will be elected to guard the essence of the project. A second board will be established that is responsible for the executive duties. Everyone is eligible for the board, but the board members will be replaced regularly, for instance every two years. To be a member of a board one must meet certain conditions pertaining to one's personal development and sincere dedication to the spiritual process. A universally oriented mind and personal qualities are also required to fulfil the position."

"This project is called the Christ Project. This does not mean that one must be a Christian in accordance with the classic religious norm in order to participate. A number of basic concepts will be formulated as essential guidelines for shaping the project. One of the aspects of this project is to bring together groups of people from various religions who are open to a universal vision in order to promote integration so that the basis of a new spirituality can be formed in which all religious and spiritual persuasions can be represented. However, one must be willing to accept that the relationship with the Divine does not belong exclusively to one particular group on Earth.

Exercise - Integration of all people and other forms of consciousness to create a network of love and light together

• Withdraw to a quiet place.

• Close your eyes and turn your attention to your breathing.

• Breathe deeply into the belly and feel how you relax.

• Turn your attention to your heart and feel the unconditional love that is in your heart.

• Let the love flow to all your cells and feel the love awaken in each cell.

• Feel the love radiate out through all your pores. You are a point of love and a point of light, like a star.

• Imagine that you are amongst people who are dear to you.

• Become aware that they are also stars, just like you. They radiate love and light. Feel how that feels.

• Connect with them so that together you are a network of light and love.

• Imagine you are in the centre of your town. Feel and see all the residents of your town.

• Become aware that they are also stars, just like you. They radiate love and light. Feel how that feels.

• Connect with them so that together you are a network of light and love.

• Imagine you are in the middle of your country. Feel and see all the people who live in your country.

• Become aware that they are also stars, just like you. They radiate love and light. Feel how that feels.

• Connect with them so that together you are a network of light and love.

• Imagine you are in the middle of your continent. Feel and see all the people who live on the continent.

• Become aware that they are also stars, just like you. They radiate love and light. Feel how that feels.

• Connect with them so that together you are a network of light and love.

• Imagine you are at the centre of your planet. Feel and see all the people who live on your planet.

• Become aware that they are also stars, just like you. They radiate love and light. Feel how that feels.

• Connect with them so that together you are a network of light and love.

• Imagine you are at the centre of your solar system. Open yourself to all the beings and forms of consciousness that exist in the solar system.

• Become aware that they are also stars, just like you. They radiate love and light. Feel how that feels.

• Connect with them so that together you are a network of light and love.

• Imagine you are at the centre of the universe. Open yourself to all the beings and forms of consciousness that exist in the universe.

• Become aware that they are also stars, just like you. They radiate love and light. Feel how that feels.

• Connect with them so that together you are a network of light and love.

• Feel this universal network of light and love of which you are a part. Become aware that you belong in this large family of love and light. Take your time to enjoy this.

• Feel how this network of light and love withdraws into your heart and integrates there. Take your time to enjoy this.

• Make contact again with your breathing in the belly and feel your body again.

• Slowly open your eyes and return to the here and now.

Repeat this exercise regularly and share it with others."

Revelation 22

The spiritual masters emphasise the personal transformation of the people who wish to participate in the Christ Project and the development of their consciousness. They explain that the various religions actually complement each other and will all have a place in the new community. "Do you think that Mohammed, Jesus, Buddha and Moses could be at variance with each other?" Exercise to accept other religions.

Mary, Jesus and Mary Magdalene: "In Revelation 21 we presented, among other things, an outline of the Christ Project. We will now say something about the contents. This project centres on the relationship between man and woman. The woman is respected and plays an essential role in healing the position of both sexes. To get this project started, women must learn to receive and men must learn to give. This circulates the energy in the relationship in the right direction (see Revelation 12)."

"The principle that everything is created from within also plays an important role. People are taking more and more responsibility for their own experiences and for what they create in their own lives; people observe themselves more and more to explore the underlying patterns that are responsible for their own behaviour and for their own manifestation in the world. A team is being formed of therapists and coaches who think and work holistically and who facilitate personal development processes at physical, energetic and psycho-emotional levels. This process will be finally completed when the role of victim is resolved, when one takes responsibility for one's own life and when unconditionality and compassion are created.

This is the basis created by Buddha, who then passed it on to Christ. The people will focus on functioning from the heart and no longer on the basis of dogmas. They will then be ready for love and for spiritual connection with higher spheres. This will also be cultivated in this community and in the project through meditation, prayer, energetic treatments and exercises that connect the physical and subtle energetic bodies with each other and purify them. All required techniques – some known, some unknown – will become available in order to let the intended process unfold completely."

Religions are complementary

"In this project, all the various esoteric aspects of today's religions are respected and practised; an awareness of the continuity and unity of all religions is awakened. People will become aware that every religion and every spiritual movement has contributed in its time to the total development of mankind. And it is the task of mankind to discover this. The messages of the various prophets and saints do not conflict; there are various complementary aspects that let mankind develop in its entirety."

"The manner in which people today deal with religions is partly at variance with the essence that the various spiritual masters wanted to convey. Every spiritual persuasion is based on love and respect for each other and encourages one to surpass the individual ego to achieve a more universal connection with everything that exists. If people use their personal ego to attack other forms of religion, something very essential is damaged in the heart, primarily in the heart of the attacker. However, the time has come to awaken, to let go of old habits and give up the need to dominate; the time has come to act with faith in love. If you think or feel that you must murder for your faith, you have no faith in God, you cut yourself off from the Divine and lapse into impotence. This is the essence of the conflicts in the world today and in the past. We call on all of mankind to make a serious decision to work together at a spiritual level, just as we do from the spiritual world. Do you perhaps think that we, the White Brother- and Sisterhood, also argue with each other? That Mohammed, Jesus, Buddha and Moses can be at variance with each other? Do you perhaps think that every religion and every master talks about a different God? If someone thinks or feels this, it is only a projection of the inner struggle of his ego and his attachment to the pattern of victim and perpetrator."

"The spiritual masters have all guided mankind lovingly and con-sciously on the path to discovery of the inner Divine essence and every one of us has used a message and a method that was the most suitable at that time in your development, at that place on Earth. We have prepared the ground for your next spiritual step. As an exam-ple: when Jesus came on Earth, Judaism, Buddhism, Hinduism and Taoism had created a basis for the arrival of the Christ-energy. When the prophet Mohammed came, Judaism and Christianity had also made preparations. As you can see, we function as one and it is time for you to do so too. One religion is just as valuable as the other; all parts together form the truth. You can put this into prac-tise by means of the following exercise."

Exercise to accept other religions

"We have a good exercise to put this into practice.

• Is there any religion or spiritual persuasion to which you have any resistance? Become aware of this.

• Draw up a list of all the negative opinions you have of that religion.

• Make contact with the higher guide of your own religion. If you are a Christian, contact Jesus Christ, for instance (you can make con-tact through visualisation, prayer, a request or by expressing the intention that you wish to make contact).

- Give this spiritual guide all the negative opinions you have listed, one by one. For each opinion you will receive unconditional love from your guide in return. This unconditional love is without judgement and gives acceptance for your personal process but no confirmation of your opinions. By transferring your negative opinions to your guide you let them go. At the moment that your guide receives them they are transformed into love.

- Draw up a list of the positive aspects that you see in the same religion; look for at least three points.

- Make contact with the guide of the religion to which you feel resistance.

- Pass on these positive aspects to this guide, one by one, with the intention of acknowledging that religion and you will receive acknowledgement from the guide in return.

- Draw up a list of steps that you can take in order to experience integration in your heart between your own religion and the religion that you initially condemned.

- Make simultaneous contact with the guide of your own religion and the guide of the other religion. Give them both the points on your list, one by one, in which you express your intention to integrate both religions in your heart. With each aspect you transfer, you acknowledge both religions at the same time. At the moment that you transfer them you will receive from the guides in return acknowledgement, unconditional love and strength to carry out your task successfully. If you so decide, you can also express your intention to inspire other people in the same process. We wish you much happiness and salvation. You have all our blessings in this process."

Revelation 23

The spiritual masters emphasise the importance of improved interaction between the 'highest' and 'lowest' chakras in our bodies in order to actually be able to experience the power of love and the Divine. Basic principles for participating in the Christ Project are formulated. Exercise to put negative opinions into perspective.

Mary, Jesus and Mary Magdalene: "We will now discuss safety. It is useful in this respect to make an imaginary energetic connection between the heart and the first chakra (see the Glossary) in the abdomen. We call this a loving connection with the basis. People feel unsafe in this day and age. This is because the norms and values that apply in current society are not attuned properly to the heart, if at all. Most norms and values people adhere to have to do with and are linked to the lower three chakras, the lower three of the seven energy centres in the human body. The first chakra is linked in this case to the survival mechanism; it is linked to fear and the belief that there is not enough for everyone. This entails mortal fear. The third chakra connects with this. It is the chakra from where people function from the ego, from power. Many try to compensate this mortal fear through the use of power. They then create for themselves the illusion of eternal life and believe that they can dominate their environment."

"The second chakra, in which human creative power is located, cannot connect its energy with the higher chakras because the creativity is monopolised by the relationship between the third and the first chakras. People occasionally try to connect with a higher state of consciousness through sexual release."

"The current state of affairs of the population on Earth is a result of this functioning. Everything is actually based on mortal fear; you are not very aware of your own Divine essence. The manner in which various religions, such as Judaism, Christianity and Islam, are professed is still often aimed at perpetuating this mistake. The religions seem to want to shape their followers with fear as the driving force and not through love as the primary motive. Many do believe in a God, but still only see little of God in themselves. To these religions, these people are not a part of God, but are closed off from God; people must be afraid of God."

"This maintains the division between the lower three chakras and the heart chakra. By nourishing and fostering the connection between the heart and the higher chakras, people become ready to realise who they really are, namely an inextricable part of God. Love thus becomes the driving force within you. It is the only way to increase the collective consciousness on Earth. At the moment that the lower three chakras surrender themselves to and connect with the heart, the following essential transformations take place:

• The first chakra makes sure that everything you do to settle on Earth takes place in accordance with ecological and respectful principles for nature and one's fellow man.
• The second chakra nourishes itself with Divine love and its creations are not only in the service of that one person but of the whole universe.
• The third chakra puts its organisational power in the service of the heart."

"When mankind arrives at this point it is connected naturally and in its entirety with higher dimensions and the Earth is positioned where it belongs, namely in its cosmic relationship as a sister of all the stars and planets in the universe. We wish to build the foundations of the Christ Project on the basis of these principles. By establishing a community that functions in accordance with these principles, a centre of light is created that has a healing effect on the whole. This changes and increases the collective vibration of the consciousness on Earth."

Principles of the Christ Project

"We will now formulate a number of principles that form the basis for participating in the Christ Project. One can exchange ideas on these principles and express one's intention to integrate them in the Christ Project. It is a dynamic process and people are constantly confronted with new challenges with respect to these principles."

1. Being responsible for one's own reality and experiences

"There are no victims and offenders. You create different realities together in order to experience them. We must bear in mind that you sometimes experience pain, stress, sorrow and anger. That is part of your personal quest on your way back to your Divine essence. It's all part of the deal. To break loose from the victim and offender consciousness you must be prepared to abolish the following:

• the need to dominate
• the need to be right
• the need to attract negative attention
• the need to bind people to you by means of guilt

This puts you in contact with your own uncertainty, with an inner feeling of emptiness and with your own vulnerability."

2. Being prepared to accept others unconditionally as they are

"Everyone needs recognition and confirmation. Sometimes you try to achieve a good feeling about yourself by condemning others. This gives a false feeling of superiority and self-confidence. By letting go of the habit of condemning others you also feel your own uncertainty and vulnerability. The beauty is that you can then see and experience others with complete acceptance for who they are as human beings. In this way you learn to accept yourself. This opens the heart to freedom and connection."

3. Becoming aware that you are immortal

"By functioning on Earth in time and space, mankind is often distracted from its true nature, namely the immortality of one's own consciousness. People have little contact with higher levels of their own consciousness. During spiritual experiences and peak experiences, people come into contact with higher states of consciousness. These higher states of consciousness give access to experiencing other dimensions. Other laws of nature apply in these dimensions than in one's normal functioning on Earth, thus making possible other experiences and insights."

"We refer to the normal consciousness on Earth as 'the third dimension'. This is a dimension in which the quality of what people experience is determined by how they experience time and space. Human thinking and feeling is geared to time and space. Everything happens at a certain moment and in a certain place. Everything on Earth is organised according to this principle. People experience reality as a sequence of events, one after the other. So thinking becomes more logical (cause and effect) than holistic (everything is connected and forms an entity)."

"All human actions in the third dimension are linked to an image that is projected from higher dimensions. Just like a film or stage director can oversee a certain movie or play, everyone's higher self (yourself in higher dimensions) has an overall picture of its own individual existence in the third dimension. Events that are sometimes inexplicable can be explained in a high-dimensional overall picture."

"People are used to looking at developments and events from the human three-dimensional perspective and are therefore not able to understand some things on Earth. Many are trained to understand everything according to the duality principle; good versus evil, beautiful versus ugly, love versus hate, welcome versus unwelcome, etc. Because they apply this duality principle they cannot grasp the whole. One way in which this duality can be transcended is to make it a habit to look at both poles at the same time. Try to picture the good and the evil of a certain event at the same time, or to experience the beautiful and the ugly at the same time. Feel what happens to you then."

"Meditation, prayer and spiritual exercises open people to experiencing oneness. The heart functions holistically, is connected with everything and experiences unity. The heart is thus the gateway to higher states of consciousness and to experiencing other dimensions. As the heart opens wider, one's consciousness grows and one comes in contact with inner wisdom and with other as yet unknown truths. One of these truths is immortality, the realisation that one's existence is not dependent on time and space or on being incarnated on Earth. Human existence is not dependent on being born or on dying."

"The next dimension to which the heart leads one is the fourth dimension. The fourth dimension is not linked to time and space. In the fourth dimension one is present everywhere at all times. One is young and old at the same time. One is here and elsewhere at the same time. One transcends the experience of duality so that it functions in connection with one's 'existing'."

"While meditating and praying and during spiritual exercises, one can 'experience' the fourth dimension, often in the form of a brief experience that has a transforming effect on the human consciousness. Experiencing these higher states of consciousness on a regular basis enables one to integrate the 'unity principle', experiencing unity above duality, in everyday life. This teaches one to act on the basis of freedom and love."

"One is then totally present in the here and now, however paradoxical that may sound. One is not absent in the mental world, but functions very practically from the heart on Earth. People have let go of many mental images, worries and fears, the tendency towards control, anger and sorrow – emotions that are linked to the three-dimensional existence in which death is a threat – and use survival tactics from the ego in order to be able to continue to exist. At the moment that one realises that nobody can actually take away one's 'existence', the human emotional experience is hugely transformed and one finally experiences freedom and peace. There are no obligations. And everything that one does do is based on inspiration and is in harmony with the whole and with oneself. Within the scope of the Christ Project this gives people the opportunity to place their actions and experiences in a broad context so that they can gradually give a practical embodiment to this four-dimensional and non-dualistic view on Earth."

Exercise - Placing negative opinions in another perspective

"By means of the following exercise you let go of the weight that you have given to various situations by integrating both the positive and the so-called negative sides of the situation in your heart. This enables you to look at your life objectively; room is created for more freedom, for putting things into perspective and for humour.

• Withdraw to a quiet place.

• Close your eyes and turn your attention to your breathing.

• Breathe deeply into the belly and feel how you relax.

• Turn your attention to a situation about which you have a negative opinion.

- Open yourself and take your time to explore, experience and feel this situation.

- Look for the positive side of the situation as well.

- Open yourself and take your time to explore, experience and feel that side of the situation as well.

- Become aware that both sides, both positive and negative, are true and that together they are an entity.

- Embrace them in your heart with compassion.

- Let the Christ-consciousness awaken in your heart. Say out loud: *"The Christ-consciousness in my heart is awake!"*

- Experience the unconditional love of your Christ-consciousness.

- Let the positive and the negative sides of the situation merge with the unconditional love of your Christ-consciousness.

- Enjoy it.

- Breathe deeply into the belly and make contact again with your body.

- Slowly open your eyes and return to the here and now."

Revelation 24

Mary and Jesus compare the parent/child relationship with the relationship between the spiritual masters and mankind. If a parent fosters his or her inner child, that parent is also better able to give his or her child love and acknowledge that child as an individual soul. Mankind has achieved increased consciousness and reveals itself more and more as a partner of the spiritual masters. Exercise to make contact with your inner child and to accept it

Mary and Jesus: "This Revelation deals with raising children and is linked to Revelation 25 that centres on the relationship of mankind with the Divine world. There is a parallel between these two topics. Children are conceived and born as a result of the attraction that they feel to their future parents at the level of their souls. Parents and children have something to work out with each other on Earth. Their relationship serves as a clear example for each other. Both parents and children are very self-centred."

"Children bring their parents into contact with their inner child. Every adult has an imaginary child within himself or herself. We call that child 'the inner child'. It is the side of the adult that still feels like a child and has remained a child. They are the 'seniors' as children. This aspect of the adult person still wants to play and have fun. It still yearns for all sorts of things, especially for love, security and attention. The inner child still has all sorts of emotions and often still needs to come to terms with them. The relationship that one used to have as children with parents or guardians has now become the relationship between the 'child side' and the 'adult side' of oneself. It is as if parents or guardians have gotten under your skin and have become a part of you. At the moment that parents get their own child, they tend to treat this child in the way that their inner child wants to be treated. This makes it difficult to appreciate the real child as it truly is. People are often only in dialogue with themselves."

"Every child that is born is in reality an adult soul that manifests itself in a small body. Every soul has its own quest on Earth, namely that which it wants to sort out, experience and realise in this incarnation. All the experiences that one undergoes in life are aimed at creating consciousness of one's own Divinity. Following the heart is the most straightforward way to become conscious of your Divinity. The Divine consciousness of people can be felt in the heart. So it is a challenge for parents to sense the intentions of the Divine consciousness of the child and to guide it on the basis of these intentions."

"As parents, people tend to treat their own children like they treat their own inner child. People raise their children like they themselves would like to be raised as a child. Furthermore, people often expect that their children's quest on Earth is the same as theirs. However, their experience of Divinity is different from the child's own experience of Divinity, just as everybody's experience of Divinity is different from their parents' experience of their own Divinity. As a result of these expectations, people are often not able to sense the Divine plan of their own children and hence miss the most essential aspect of their responsibility."

The relationship between parent and child

"During conception, a spiritual unification occurs between the parents and the soul of the child. A flow of love that becomes increasingly more profound develops with this unification. Parents have two responsibilities with respect to their children. These are symbolised in the form of a cross. The vertical line symbolises guiding the relationship between the child and its higher self and the horizontal line symbolises guiding the relationship between the child and society."

"Many dilemmas arise in the relationship between parents and children. As parents, people sometimes feel that the demands of the society in which the child takes part and the stimuli of the child's Divine plan, in which the spiritual fulfilment of the child manifests itself, seem to conflict. However, this dilemma is automatically resolved when the two forces are integrated. By listening to both forces at the same time and by following them, a new reality and a new consciousness are created in which the child should grow. The parents grow, too, in a process that runs parallel to that of their child and they achieve new forms of integration between their Divine consciousness and society. Enjoy it and experience it as light-heartedly as possible without losing focus. If one is aware and disengaged it is much easier to walk the path of love. Should you want personal instruction and guidance in this, do not hesitate to pray to us. We have a lot of experience in this."

"A dual form of parenthood develops in the relationship between children and parents, namely from parents towards children and from parents towards themselves. Adults must guide their children in their development and must develop themselves in their new role of parent. As parents, people are faced with two processes. They are faced, on the one hand, with all the concrete aspects that ensue from guiding children and on the other hand with all the unresolved emotional processes that children stir up in them. This occurs under the influence of the mirror that children hold up to their parents. Because the more one is able to love oneself and completely accept one's inner child, the more one is able to accept one's own children unconditionally and let them be who they really are. The love for one's child and the love for oneself develop together. The children help their parents open their hearts. The more one surrenders to this process, the more this relationship will resemble one's relationship with the spiritual world. In this relationship, the spiritual world guides everyone in the relationship with one's own Divinity but then without projections."

The guidance of the masters will change

"Perhaps you have noticed that our tasks run in parallel. Because mankind is now in a stage in which it is able to take up its own responsibility, our guidance is changing. Mankind is growing and becoming our partner to an increasingly greater extent. And in the same way, as children grow intellectually, they become partners of their parents to an ever greater extent. At a certain stage, they need hardly any guidance any longer; they have come to the point that they can do things on their own. This will also happen at some time between us, the spiritual masters, and you, mankind. At some stage, people will even take over our duties. We will then be able to take on other tasks, like you do when your children leave home. The Christ Project represents, as it were, mankind's 'living-in-digs period'. From there, people can create a new reality that comprises something new, a style of its own and elements of what one has learned up to then, but that on an essential level is geared to a higher consciousness. We see this project like parents see their children when they live in digs. You see that they are building up something new and consider that a challenge. They occasionally find it difficult to fit that into their way of life, but at the same time it brings refreshingly new possibilities. If you are honest and dare to listen to your feelings, you will realise that this growth process is what you have longed for for so long."

Exercice - Contact with your inner child

"The following exercise brings you in loving contact with your inner child and with your own children and other people.

• Withdraw to a quiet place.

- Close your eyes and turn your attention to your breathing.

- Breathe deeply into the belly and feel how you relax.

- Turn your attention to your heart and feel the unconditional love that is in your heart. Feel the total acceptance of who you are.

- Open yourself to receive the unconditional love of the White Brother- and Sisterhood in your heart and feel our total acceptance of who you are.

- Let yourself be borne by the love.

- Send the unconditional love that is in your heart to all the cells of your body.

- Become conscious of your inner child and feel where he/she is in your body.

- Send the unconditional love that is in your heart to your inner child and feel your total acceptance of who he/she is.

- Feel how your inner child feels borne by your love.

- Feel the connection of the heart that you have with your own children. If you do not have children, select someone else with whom you have a connection of the heart.

- Send the unconditional love that is in your heart to your child or to the other person and feel your total acceptance of who he/she is.

- Feel how your child/that person feels borne by your love.

- Become conscious of the connection of the heart that your child/that person has with someone else.

• Visualise and feel how your child or the other person sends the unconditional love that is in his/her heart to someone else and feel the total acceptance of this person.

• Become conscious of the connection of the heart that this person has with someone else.

• Visualise and feel how this person sends the unconditional love that is in his/her heart to someone else and feel the total acceptance of this person.

• Become conscious of the connection of the heart that this person has with someone else.

• Visualise and feel how this person sends the unconditional love that is in his/her heart to someone else and feel the total acceptance of this person.

• Continue until you feel and see all of mankind create a network of unconditional love and acceptance and you feel the wave of love flow back to you.

• Take your time to enjoy this.

• Turn your attention back to your breathing.

• Feel your body again.

• Slowly open your eyes and return to the here and now."

Revelation 25

Mary and Jesus tell about the special relationship between the spiritual masters and mankind. The spiritual masters occasionally wonder whether they should 'save' people from the situations in life that they have created themselves or whether they should let them experience them to the full from the point of view of the evolutionary process. The answer is provided by the Divine plan. It is time for people to take responsibility for what they create and learn to make other choices. Mankind and the masters can then be partners. Exercise as an aid for consciously deciding whether or not you want to be a victim in this life.

Mary and Jesus: "The interaction between mankind and the 'spiritual Divine world' (the immaterial level of Divine love) is a special relationship. People expect the spiritual guides to solve and create all sorts of things for them and are angry or disappointed when this does not happen. If it does happen, people can be thankful for a time, but after a while they have forgotten it again. People ask us for all sorts of advice and guidance, but when we give it to them they often do not listen or it does not meet their expectations. They create all sorts of situations and circumstances of their own accord and distance themselves from them later on. Sometimes we also wonder how to deal with these situations. To what extent should we support people in experiencing created situations that damage or hurt them? To what extent should we let people experience that? To what extent should we restrain them from damaging themselves? To what extent should we either support them in their process or not get involved at all? We synchronise ourselves with someone's Divine plan and that makes it perfectly clear. Sometimes there are situations in which the person in question wishes to experience his or her own power of destruction to the full or must feel, experience and live through the consequences of his or her own aggression, arrogance and ambition. This ultimately enables one to make different choices later on."

Not constantly saving people

"We have a lot of compassion and love for mankind. We also have an eye for everyone's need to experiment in life; that is what you have come on Earth for, but there are also limits to these experiments. You see, mankind is not alone in the universe. There are also other forms of life and consciousness that one must learn to respect. In most cases, this takes care of itself as a result of the interaction between man and nature and between man and the Cosmos. However, sometimes it is necessary to intervene from the spiritual world. This can be the case when people try to do things that have implications for a region, a territory or an aspect of life that are larger than what mankind is entitled to. Sometimes the restriction comes from within because one is not able to function at a level of consciousness that one has not yet been able to achieve. People create certain situations, but then do not wish to accept the consequences of their experiences. So they ask us to save them from these experiences whereas that is not always possible. We can send them love and strength, we can support them, but the people themselves must solve the problems they have brought upon themselves. We cannot keep on 'saving' them; rather, we let them fully experience 'being the victim' of the experiences they created themselves."

Light-hearted transformation of consciousness

"The only way in which mankind can experience peace and love is for people to take responsibility for the situations in life that they have created themselves and learn to make the right decisions. Mankind is more advanced in its development and is no longer treated as helpless children but as independent beings who are able to create and choose. People are already able to realise what the consequences are of their decisions and the situations in life they create, both for themselves and for their environment, and to take responsibility for them. This is a transformation of consciousness that can occur in a light-hearted way. It is one's own decision whether it is a light-hearted or a difficult transformation. The more people resist this inevitable truth, the more difficult it becomes. The more people are prepared to surrender to this transformation and trust and accept both themselves and us, the more lively, light-hearted and loving this process unfolds."

On the road back from the deepest point

"What is the nature of our relationship with the people on Earth? We are ready to help you and support you in anything you wish. We also give you all the freedom you want to experience yourself within the above-mentioned limits. We are unconditionally at the service of mankind, that is to say that we do not judge and do not expect anything in return. We are an example for mankind. In essence, people are just like us, namely God. Only they have forgotten this. At a certain moment on the way back to rediscovering their Divine essence, the people will meet up with us and then we can become one and play, develop, work and grow together in the playground of the universe. We are here to remind the people of their Divine essence to the extent to which they wish to be reminded. The Earth is a free-will zone; it is a special zone that has been created to enable everyone to experience his or her free will, that is to say that everyone is free to create and to experience the consequences of their own free will. In that process, you learn to choose. Just like a child learns to walk and move, you learn to deal with the reality you created yourself. You are ready to take this step."

"The consciousness on Earth used to be much lower. There have also been times on this planet when the collective human consciousness was at a higher level; however, it then dropped and now you are on your way back from the deepest point. That was just before the arrival of Jesus Christ on Earth and since then there has been an upward trend. During the two world wars there were temporary dips. You then 'played' with forces that could destroy the entire Earth. We are now in a period of recovery; you are opening yourselves more and more to your own essence. When the consciousness on Earth was lower, we had a different relationship with mankind. We could only give love and support, help to heal wounds and make contact with the few who were prepared to open themselves to us. Now that you are more developed we can develop a certain kind of partnership. To give this partnership more meaning you must be prepared to take responsibility for your own Divinity. We will then be able to work together to a much greater extent."

Exercise - To be or not to be a victim

"The following exercise will help you become aware of your role as the creator of your life. It will also help you to decide whether you want to continue your experience of being a victim or whether you wish to let go of it.

• Withdraw to a quiet place.

• Close your eyes and turn your attention to your breathing.

• Breathe deeply into the belly and feel how you relax.

• Select a situation in your life in which you feel you are a victim.

• Breathe deeply into the belly and feel how it feels to feel a victim in this situation.

- Imagine that instead of being a victim you are the creator of this situation.

- Look at and experience the situation again as its creator.

- Breathe deeply into the belly and feel how it feels to feel like the creator of this situation.

- Experience this without judging.

- Become conscious of the positive things that you get out of this situation.

- Become conscious of the sacrifices you must make to maintain this situation.

- Feel in your heart whether you want to continue to create this situation.

- Make a conscious decision to either continue to create this situation or to stop.

- Breathe deeply into the belly and feel how your decision feels.

- Open your eyes and return to the here and now."

Epilogue by the White Brother- and Sisterhood

Dear people on Earth,

It is with much joy that we have arrived at the end of this book. It is our gift to inspire you and to help you open your hearts; in the first place for yourselves, so that you may love yourself as a Divine creature, and in the second place to love others, other living creatures and the Earth as a part of God. The essence of our message is that love is everything and everything is love. This means that love is what the world revolves around. Even people's most illogical and inexplicable actions are motivated by the search for love. There is nothing else but love in the world. And love is God and God is love. So there is nothing else in the world but God and God is everything. Sometimes you become frightened and you forget this universal principle. The purpose of this book is to remind you that you are love and God. Love is the all-embracing force and motive of all human deeds.

Besides our message to 'love yourself', we have another message, namely 'fraternise yourself'. That is to say, connect with others, let others into your heart, let others touch you, and also be there for others, without neglecting or hurting yourself. Look for trust, build up trust together. Mutual trust can be built up on the basis of respect and by taking each other's needs into consideration. Mutual trust is a fine basis for working well together and giving meaning to your being together. It is a basis for a non-violent world. As you work on this, we will collaborate with you to an ever greater extent and we will become more and more one, so that at a certain moment all of mankind will have become part of the White Brother- and Sisterhood. At that moment, people will take over our tasks and we will turn to more universal assignments to connect the Earth with the Cosmos. Some of you will abandon your physical form during the course of this process and collaborate with us directly from the spiritual dimension. To stimulate this process of ongoing brother- and sisterhood, we now give you one more instruction. With every drastic event, such as a murder or an attack, also give attention to the cause, to the antipole that has caused this event. Look for the integration of the antipoles, look at the whole, do not polarise. Only through the integration of all the antipoles will there be peace. People must learn to be more considerate of each other. There is plenitude and everyone is entitled to be themselves, to satisfy their own needs, but at the same time they must also have respect for the others and their needs. Satisfying the needs of an individual or a group may never cause pain and the suppression of others. See God in the other as well. God is everyone and everyone is God. There is no single person or group that can claim exclusivity. No one can take away another person's Divinity. Even if you cause each other emotional, mental or physical pain, you cannot take away each other's Divinity, not even your own. The idea that you can damage someone else or yourself is only an illusion. The process of liberation and learning, all the events and experiences you need to discover that you are God, is what keeps you in the cycle of reincarnation – of dying and being born again on Earth – and what is also called karma. You are now in an accelerating process of the opening of the heart. New things keep happening; confrontational situations and unexpected challenges that help you to come more into the heart in a short period of time. Your higher self, the Divine consciousness that everyone has, has decided at a collective level to take a great leap forward during the coming years. In order to accomplish this, everyone has a customised learning programme in life. Take everything that happens as a gift of God, take it with love and acceptance, no matter how difficult it can sometimes be. Continue to trust, continue to trust your higher self, continue to trust God and continue to trust us.

In love we are together,
The White Brother- and Sisterhood

Glossary

Dimensions of consciousness
The universe is made up not only of 'space', such as the different solar and stellar systems, but also of levels of consciousness. Each level of consciousness contains a different experience of the universe and of life. The higher the level, the broader and more profound the experience and the insight of the beings that are at that level of consciousness. These beings have a much better insight into and overview of all sorts of events in the universe. They act, if necessary, from this higher level of insight. The higher the level of consciousness, the more profoundly one experiences the Divine consciousness. Each level of consciousness has its own laws of nature that control the experiences in the specific dimension. Examples of levels of consciousness are:

The third dimension
This is the level of most people on Earth. They function according to the principle of duality. That is to say that they divide everything into two poles in order to understand, place and classify everything. The greatest division is between good and evil. They experience resistance as a result of this division. That is to say that they mainly want the 'good' and feel resistance towards 'evil'. Experiencing resistance keeps them in pain and fear and maintains an inner division. Only by healing this division and by accepting both the 'good' and the 'evil' in themselves can they obtain access to a broader view of life. Then they will rise above death and birth and obtain access to the fourth dimension.

The fourth dimension

This is the dimension above time and space. There is no time and no space there. Those who function at that level of consciousness can experience all places and all times simultaneously. They feel young and old at the same time, at home and far away at the same time. They experience the unity of everything. They have no obligations.

The fifth dimension

This is the dimension of compassion, unconditional love and acceptance of everything as being a part of the Divine plan, as being a Divine play.

The sixth dimension

Wisdom and insight into all laws of nature. Being able to operate according to the Divine plan at all levels. Profound insight into one's own Divine being. Experience of the unity between one's self and everything.

The seventh dimension

Oneness with God. One's self is entirely merged with the Divine.

Extraterrestrial forms of consciousness and entities

These are forms of consciousness that come to us from beyond Earth. People are often observed by other beings from all ends of the universe. Several of these beings are involved in the development of mankind for their own development process as well. Several races, civilisations and population groups are not yet conscious of their extraterrestrial relationship and origin. They are connected directly with specific stellar systems such as the Pleiades or Orion.

Chakras

Energetic centres that connect the physical body with the subtle bodies. Life exists under a tension between the heavenly and the earthly energies. The integration of these two energies is perpetuated by the chakras. This connection takes place in the midline of our body close to the spinal cord. The vibration of the chakras is higher towards the top of our head and lower towards the genitals. They are linked to essential physiological processes and processes of consciousness. They help to digest all sorts of new influences and to master them. People can thus give all sorts of experiences a place in their lives. There are also chakras outside the physical body that have more subtle functions. A great deal of literature is available on the chakras and can be consulted to expand on this brief description.

Energetic forms of consciousness
Not all forms of consciousness have a physical body. Some have only an energetic body. An energetic body vibrates at a higher frequency than a physical body and cannot be perceived by most people. Some people have opened subtle powers of perception within themselves and can perceive these beings by seeing, feeling and/or hearing them.

Intergalactic light beings
Beings that are consciously connected with the Divine plan at a high level, at an intergalactic level. They operate to help manifest and coordinate the Divine plan in multiple stellar systems. They often have coordinating, inspiring and protective functions. They are part of the network of the light.

Holy Spirit
This is the manifestation of the Divine will. When God wants to create something, God does this via the Holy Spirit. It is the process of creation between the Creator and what is created. The Holy Spirit comprises infinite love and compassion. Each creation comes to be by means of a process of Divine Love. Everything that exists is basically pure love.

Higher self
People on Earth are usually in contact with their minor self, namely the 'self' they experience in this third dimension. They experience themselves as their minor 'me'. But people also have a self that func-

tions in higher dimensions and that they often do not try to contact. This 'higher self', the soul at a higher level of consciousness, is aware of the Divine in mankind and feels connected with everything. When people want to, they can call up this 'higher self' for guidance and to experience the events in life on Earth from a more profound perspective. Contact with the higher self also brings people in contact with higher laws of nature so that everything in their lives begins to flow and life becomes increasingly easier for them.

Intergalactic order

Harmony, structure and coordinated interaction between the various stellar systems. This is perpetuated by the Intergalactic Council of High Light Beings, Masters of Wisdom.

Network of the light

Network of beings who are attuned to the Divine love and the Divine plan. They collaborate to help restore the consciousness of the Divine in the third dimension on Earth. They promote the awakening of the Christ-energy on Earth and in other dimensions.

Prayers

Almighty God
I ask you
In the name of your son, Jesus Christ
Have mercy upon me
Amen

(optional)
Have mercy upon me and help me with ....

Lord Jesus Christ
Son of God
Have mercy upon me
Amen

Dear Mary Magdalene
Divine woman
Have mercy upon me and awaken in me
Help me to heal and appreciate the female principle within
me
In all the depths of my being, in my fellow man and in
everything on Earth
Amen

Dear Mary
Divine mother of Heaven and Earth
Have mercy upon me
Awaken the love in my heart for all that exists and for
myself
Help me to live with an open mind like a Divine child
That is amazed about everything
And that treats everything in this Heavenly paradise with
love and respect
Help me to let my Divine essence awaken completely
To be who I actually am in Heaven and on Earth
And that your love and my love, dear Mother, may be one
For now and forever
Amen

Dear Christ
Who is present in my heart
Awaken in me
And through me
In everything that exists
Amen

Dear God
Mother and Father God
All-embracing power that is in my heart
Awaken in me
And help me so that I at all times in my life
In every word, with every deed and act
Will be aware of my Divinity
Help me to manifest the Divine love on Earth
And with me in every fellow man
Amen

(a)
Dear Heavenly Father
And all the unconditional guides, masters, angels and higher souls of the universe,
I feel, look at and listen to you with all due love and respect
Because I know
That we have been created out of the same Divine love.
We are one!

(b)
Dear Heavenly Mother
And all gentle powers of the universe
And Mother Nature
With all her plants, animals and creatures,
I feel, look at and listen to you with all due love and respect
Because I know
That we have been created out of the same Divine love.
We are one!

(c)
Dear brothers and sisters of the universe,
Of all the stars and planets and various dimensions,
I feel, look at and listen to you with all due love and respect
Because I know
That we have been created out of the same Divine love.
We are one!

(d)
Dear people
Who are together here on Earth,
I feel, look at and listen to you with all due love and respect
Because I know
That we have been created out of the same Divine love.
We are one!

(e)
Dear Heavenly Mother and Father,
Dear brothers and sisters of the universe,
Dear people on Earth,
We are one!
Amen

About the authors

Gabriela and Reint Gaastra-Levin

Gabriela Levin (b. 1960) studied medicine, specialising in psychiatry and psychotherapy, at the University of Buenos Aires. In 1986, after graduating as psychiatrist, she started her own practice as an anthroposophic doctor and psychotherapist in Argentina's capital city. In 1990, at the age of thirty and after spending six months in India, she settled in the Netherlands. She studied Chinese medicine, reiki and the Indian method of treatment called Ayurveda. She practices as an Ayurvedic physician and psychotherapist. She also lectures at various medical training institutes.

Reint Gaastra (b. 1956) studied law at the University of Utrecht in the Netherlands. Upon completing his studies he joined Centraal Beheer Verzekeringen, an insurance company, in 1981. In 1988 he switched over to a publishing house, Kluwer Bedrijfsinformatie, where in 1991 he was appointed editor in chief of *ELAN*, a magazine for CEO's and non-executives. Since 1997 he has worked as an independent communication trainer and conference chairman in addition to his main activities as a journalist, columnist and part time and interim editor in chief of magazines.

Gabriela and Reint are now busy leaving step by step 'the old beautiful work' behind them and create more space and time to give lectures and workshops in the field of 'The Divinity of Mankind'.

Contact

The authors Gabriela and Reint Gaastra-Levin like to keep in touch with the readers of their books. They provide a digital newsletter for free every month with new revelations and news about their activities.

If you want to receive this Follow Your Heart – newsletter send an email to info@divinityofmankind.com or to info@followyourheart.nl

Gabriela and Reint also want to advice their readers to look regularly at their website www.divinityofmankind.com for new revelations and developments.

Contents Part II

The book 'The Divinity of Mankind – Revelations by Mary, Jesus and Mary Magdalene Part II' is already published in Belgium and The Netherlands. The publisher is working on an 'English' translation now and expects to bring this beautiful book to the world market in the period between the end of the year 2005 and the beginning of 2006.

In Part II Mary Magdalene and Jesus explain that they have had four children and tell us the way they raised them, they give advice to the people of the Earth how to raise their own children. They speak about how to love the inner child in every human being and about the holiness of sexuality. Jesus shares his deeper experiences during the Crucifixion and his Resurrection, which was not a resurrection as we think it was.
Jesus describes the true meaning of Christmas, his Ascension and Pentecost and what exactly happened when he was baptist by John. Mary, Jesus and Mary Magdalene explain the true meaning of baptism and give a beautiful baptism-ritual for all mankind. They give food for thought about not judging ourselves, compassion, forgiveness, gratefulness and enlightenment, about the essence of opening our hearts and how to do that. They explain how people create their own lives and how respect for women creates abundance. They tell us with which eyes to read the Bible and about the developments in Christian Church and Islam. Part II is also filled with new exercises and prayers.

How to order

The book 'The Divinity of Mankind – Revelations by Mary, Jesus and Mary Magdalene – Part I' (ISBN 90-807478-3-1) can be ordered worldwide via www.divinityofmankind.com, www.booksurge.com and www.amazon.com

Part II will be published in the period between the end of 2005 and the beginning of 2006.

Also the original Dutch books 'Over de Goddelijkheid van de mens – Openbaringen van Maria, Jezus en Maria Magdalena Deel I' (ISBN 90-807478-1-5) and 'Over de Goddelijkheid van de mens – Openbaringen van Maria, Jezus en Maria Magdalena Deel II' (ISBN 90-807478-2-3) can be ordered via these websites and via the Dutch website www.openbaringen.com